NEW FRONTIERS NATURAL FOODS is a family of five stores and an organic farm. Our farm and our home office are located on the Central Coast of California, as are our Solvang and San Luis Obispo stores. Our Northern Arizona stores can be found in Flagstaff, Prescott and Sedona.

We find great enjoyment and a deep sense of purpose through serving and being part of the small communities in which we live and do business. We like to think of our stores as a place where people grow, and our slogan is "We're all about your quality of life."

It's rewarding for us to share this wonderful cookbook with you, and we hope that Anne's incredible passion for cooking will inspire your passion and enhance your quality of life. We would love for you to visit us whenever you're in one of our towns.

Sincere thanks from the Folks at New Frontiers

ANNE BUNCH lives in the Santa Ynez Valley, on California's Central Coast, where she has been cooking for many years. She gained recognition for her talent in the early 1990's while she was chef at the renowned Side Street Cafe in Los Olivos, California. Anne later joined New Frontiers and uses her cooking abilities to create flavorful and appealing dishes, often using alternative ingredients for people with food allergies or dietary restrictions.

Anne is the author of a previous recipe book, "Dancing With Garlic," which is no longer in print.

HARVEST RICE - P. 43

A Muse
Came to Dinner

A Muse
Came to Dinner

Recipes of Inspiration by

Anne Bunch

Missy Collier

and

New Frontiers Natural Foods

Illustrations by

Betty Seaman

A Muse Came to Dinner

Design and layout by Missy Collier and Betty Seaman
Edited by Ann Wilson

Published by New Frontiers Holdings, Inc.
For information contact New Frontiers,
1984 Old Mission Dr., Suite A-7, Solvang CA 93463

For mail order information, see page 199

Printed in the United States of America.

Library of Congress Cataloging-in-Publication Data
pending

ISBN 0-941848-11-6

First printing, 2001
Second printing, 2003
Third printing, 2005
Fourth printing, 2008
Fifth printing, 2010

Acknowledgments

To everyone at New Frontiers: Thank you for your faith in my cooking abilities and giving me the "carte blanche" to create a deli where the food is unique, delicious and wholesome. This freedom is what allows me to draw on God's Gift to me.

Warmest thanks to so many friends: Supporters, encouragers, counselors, dreamers, fun lovers, mothers, sisters, teenagers, tasters, testers, walkers, hikers, swimmers, beach lizards, poets, bookworms, jokesters, teasers, editors, cooks, carpenters, gardeners, neighbors, waitresses, artists, huggers, visionaries, bankers, mechanics, shoppers, party givers and prayer partners.

Anne

MUSE *(myooz)* n: 1. Greek Mythology. Any of the nine daughters of Zeus, each of whom presided over a different art or science. 2. a source of inspiration; *especially:* a guiding spirit

a guiding spirit...

Dedication

To God from whom all blessings flow
To our children and their children, the joy of our lives
To all our patrons
Thank you!

LOVE is patient, love is kind.
It does not envy, it does not boast, it is not proud.
It is not rude, it is not self- seeking, it is not easily angered,
it keeps no record of wrongs.
Love does not delight in evil but rejoices with the truth.
It always protects, always trusts, always hopes, always perseveres.
—Corinthians 13: 4-7

For many, delicious cooking is a craft thought to be unachievable or requiring years of learning. For others cooking has become a daily drudgery one must endure because, let's face it, there's no getting around it, we must eat! Rare are the homes these days, where the familiar aromas of the day's prepared meals fill the rooms. Whether it be a day spent canning summer peaches, making strawberry jam, garden vegetable soup or the Sunday roast — such memorable fragrances have become an exception in the modern home.

My children refuse the partaking of Thanksgiving dinner at someone else's house for the simple reason that they look forward to the aromas, which remind that "this is home".

Cooking ought never to become mundane for the very reason that it is vital to our well-being. Such is food to the body as is food to the spirit. Therefore a little sacred time set aside to prepare food with love will benefit all who surround you, including yourself and not only your body but your total self.

I have taken the "Love" chapter from the Holy Scriptures and used some of its components as an application to inspire everyone to a different, more positive attitude towards cooking.

Let Love be your Muse and open the door to wonderful dishes which are easy to prepare, good to eat and send a message which says "I love you".

Anne

Contents

The Meditation of Cooking

After the very first breath we take upon arriving on earth, we are encouraged to eat. It is natural for the mother to bring her child to the breast to nurse. This action encompasses all the basic needs her newborn requires: nourishment of body, heart, mind and spirit.

In the course of growing up, that wholeness of nourishment is divided into different categories.

We eat physical foods to uphold the body, we receive emotional and mental support from other humans and our spiritual food comes from God. During this development, the focus of feeding our bodies is left somewhere by the wayside. We do not always honor our bodies with the fullness of nutriments needed to function optimally. Unfortunately, we do not always harvest the consequences of our mindless eating until we are quite a way down our journey, as youth has its built-in bank of seemingly endless energy. Yet it is imperative to replenish this storage with complete foods:

1. Foods that are grown in healthy circumstances, in rich soil, without added chemicals and with all the sun they require to develop their maximum nutritional qualities.

2. Foods that have been prepared with purpose and love.

This book contains some thoughts on how to bring a mindful, loving attitude to food preparation, resulting in wholeness of nourishment. Cooking with love will add that extra magical and secret ingredient resulting in happy, healthy bodies.

The recipes are for dishes that have delighted many customers at the New Frontiers Natural Foods Deli in Solvang, California.

Allow your time of cooking to become a time of setting aside the troubles and anxieties of the day—they'll be there when you return. Let this time become a time of prayer, or worship, or looking inward, or of thankfulness, and be mindful of each step and each ingredient because each meal prepared with love will make for all around satisfaction, beginning with yourself.

Anne

Soups

"Good painting is like good cooking; it can be tasted,
but not explained."

—Maurice de Vlaminck

Potato Leek Soup

Heat the broth in a large soup pot. Add the leeks and the potatoes. Return to a boil, cover and simmer until the vegetables are very soft, about 15-20 minutes. Add the pepper. Puree the soup using blender or food processor until smooth. Add the chopped parsley, the half-and-half or creamer, and salt to taste.

1 qt. (4 cups) vegetable broth
4 large leeks, washed thoroughly, chopped (white and a little green only)
1 lb. russet potatoes (about 3 medium), peeled and diced
½ tsp. ground black pepper
¼ cup parsley, finely chopped
½ cup half-and-half or Silk soymilk creamer
Salt to taste

Cheese Tortellini, Spinach and Tomato Soup

1 qt. (4 cups) vegetable broth
1 tbl. dried basil
6 garlic cloves, minced
1 medium onion, finely chopped
1 large carrot, peeled and diced
2 ribs celery, finely diced

1 28-oz. can crushed tomatoes
16-oz. store-bought cheese
  tortellini (frozen is best)

2 cups cleaned spinach, coarsely
  chopped

Shredded Parmesan cheese for
  topping

Bring the vegetable broth to a boil in a large soup pot. Add the basil, garlic, onion, carrot and celery. Cover and simmer until the vegetables are tender, approximately 10 minutes. Add the tomatoes and the tortellini. Cover and simmer until the tortellini are tender, about 8-10 minutes, depending on variety. Add the spinach. The heat of the soup will wilt the spinach; no further cooking is required. Serve with shredded Parmesan.

page of lettuce leaves?

red leaf

Roman

spinach

green leaf

arugula yum!

weird wirey stuff that everyone picks out of thier Salad.

ideas, ideas, ideas...

Golden Harvest Butternut Squash Cream Soup

Preheat oven to 350°

Prepare a baking sheet with a light coating of oil.

Place the butternut squash halves cut side down on the baking sheet and bake until they are soft to the touch, approximately 30 to 40 minutes.

Allow the squash to cool and scrape out the flesh into a bowl.

While the squash is roasting, prepare the soup. Heat the vegetable broth to a boil. Add the onion, garlic and Herbs de Provence. Simmer, covered, until onion is very soft. Add the squash pulp and heat through. Puree the soup using blender or food processor. Return the mixture to the soup pot and add the cream or the soy. Stir to blend and reheat if necessary. To avoid curdling, do *not* boil. Adjust seasoning to taste with the salt and pepper.

This is a delicious soup to serve as dinner with assorted cheeses, old-fashioned country bread and a salad.

Vegetable or olive oil

4 lbs. butternut squash, cut in half, seeded, and membranes removed

2½ quarts (10 cups) vegetable broth (homemade or commercial)

1 medium onion, chopped

8 cloves garlic, minced

1 tbl. Herbs de Provence

2 cups heavy whipping cream or 1 pint Silk soymilk creamer

Salt and pepper to taste.

Belgian Carrot Soup

1 lb. carrots, (about 4 cups) peeled and diced
1 lb. potatoes, (about 3 medium) peeled and diced
2 tbl. butter
3½ cups vegetable broth
2½ cups milk, heated
½ cup heavy cream
Salt and pepper to taste
2 tbl. chopped parsley

Melt the butter in a soup pot and gently cook the carrots and potatoes over low heat, without browning, stirring often, about ten minutes.

Add the broth to the vegetables and heat slowly to bring to a boil. Reduce the heat and simmer covered for 20-25 minutes, or until vegetables are soft. Puree, using blender or food processor. Add hot milk and season with salt and pepper to taste and simmer very slowly for 10 minutes longer. Remove from heat; stir in cream.

Sprinkle each serving with chopped parsley.

Yield: 9 cups

Dragon's Breath Tofu Soup

2½ quarts (10 cups) vegetable broth

¾ cup tamari

2 tbl. toasted sesame oil

5 cloves garlic, pressed

3 oz. fresh (only) ginger peeled and pressed (as garlic in garlic press)

1 medium onion, finely chopped

3 ribs of celery, finely diced

1 carrot, peeled and diced

1 tbl. crushed red chilies

1 medium red bell pepper seeded, membranes removed and cut in fine julienne

3 oz. Shitake mushrooms, stems removed and sliced

2 cups Napa cabbage, shredded

4 oz. bean sprouts

1 lb. extra firm tofu, drained and cubed into ½-inch pieces.

1 cup chopped cilantro

½ cup sliced green onion

Heat the broth in a large soup pot. Add the tamari, sesame oil, garlic, ginger, onion, celery, carrot and crushed red chilies. Bring to a boil, cover, and simmer until the vegetables are tender.

Add the red bell pepper, mushrooms, and the Napa cabbage.

Return to a boil, reduce heat and simmer 5 minutes longer. Add the bean sprouts and tofu and simmer long enough to heat the tofu through.

Serve with the cilantro and the green onions.

A fiery hot, healthy and exotic soup.

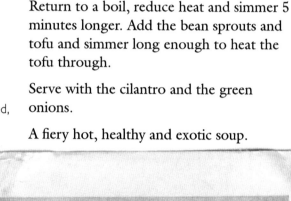

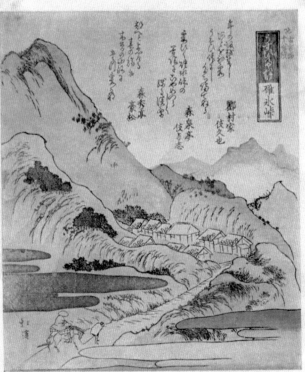

Pumpkin and Chipotle Pepper Cream Soup

If using fresh pumpkins, cut them in half and remove the seeds and membranes.

Place the halves cut side down on a greased cookie sheet and bake at 350° until they are soft, about 30-45 minutes. Scrape the flesh out of the pumpkin halves and puree using blender or food processor. Set aside.

In a large soup pot, heat the vegetable broth. Add the chopped onion and cook until soft. Add the pumpkin, the chipotle, salt, cinnamon and maple syrup. Bring to simmer over low heat, stirring frequently to prevent burning on the bottom. Remove from flame when the soup has reached a boil. Puree the soup using a blender or food processor. Return to pot, add cream or soy, and heat gently. Adjust seasonings to taste. Serve with chopped green onion, cilantro and red bell pepper sprinkled on top.

Makes 3 qts.

2 sugarpie pumpkins or 5 cups of canned pumpkin puree (1 large and 1 small can)

2 quarts of your favorite vegetable broth (*Imagine* brand is very suitable for this soup and is available in natural food stores)

1 medium onion chopped

1 whole chipotle pepper in adobo sauce (available in the Mexican section of most grocery stores) seeds removed but not necessary

Salt to taste

½ tsp. cinnamon

2 tbl. maple syrup

2 cups heavy whipping cream or 1 pint Silk soymilk creamer for vegan soup

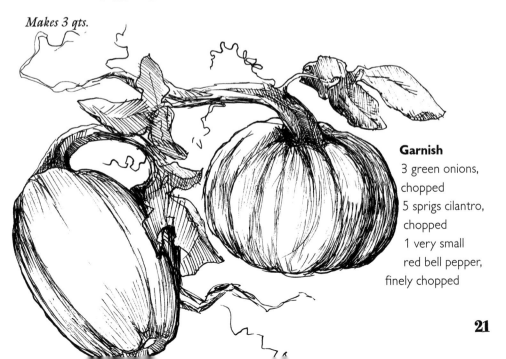

Garnish
3 green onions, chopped
5 sprigs cilantro, chopped
1 very small red bell pepper, finely chopped

Santa Fe Black Bean and Corn Soup

1½ qts. (6 cups) vegetable broth
1½ cups dried black beans, sorted
   and rinsed
1 large onion, finely chopped
6 cloves garlic, minced
2 carrots, peeled and diced small
1 small red bell pepper, seeded,
   membranes removed and diced
1 small green bell pepper, seeded,
   membranes removed and diced
1 jalapeño pepper, seeded, finely
   chopped
1 12-oz. jar chunky salsa
1 cup fresh or frozen corn
2 tsp. ground cumin

1 tsp. oregano
2 tsp. chili powder
Salt to taste
Cilantro, chopped
Green onion, sliced

In a large soup pot cook the black beans, onions, seasonings and 1 tsp. salt in the broth. Cover the pot and simmer the beans over low heat until they are soft; about 1½ hours. Add the carrot, peppers and jalapeño: simmer till soft. Add the salsa and the corn. Heat. Adjust salt to taste. Serve with the cilantro and the green onion.

Makes about 7 cups

The Pueblo Storyteller

Cream of Portabella Mushroom Soup

Bring the broth to a boil in a large soup pot. Chop the well-cleaned stems of the mushrooms. Add mushrooms to broth along with onions and thyme. Cover and simmer until soft. Puree, using blender or food processor. Return to heat and add the diced mushroom caps. Cook until tender.

Stir the flour and water into a paste, dissolving all the clumps. While stirring, pour the flour/water mixture into the soup to thicken. Cook over low heat stirring constantly for 3 minutes. Season with salt and pepper. Add cream and stir. Add parsley and chives.

1 qt. (4 cups) vegetable broth
2 lbs. Portabella mushrooms, stems removed and set aside. Using a sharp knife cut away the black flesh underneath the cap and toss. Rinse and dice mushroom caps into nickel size pieces
1 medium sweet onion, finely chopped
1 tsp. thyme
¼ cup flour
⅓ cup cold water
Salt and pepper to taste
1 cup cream, or Silk soymilk creamer for a vegan soup
2 tbl. chopped parsley
2 tbl. chopped chives

Chicken Noodle Soup

2 quarts (8 cups) water
3 bouillon cubes of your choice
1½ lbs. boneless chicken breasts
1 medium onion, chopped
3 celery ribs, finely diced
2 carrots, peeled and finely diced
Small bunch of parsley, chopped,
  divided
Salt and pepper to taste
3 oz. spaghetti noodles, broken
  in fourths

In a large soup pot, bring the water and the bouillon cubes to a boil.

Add the chicken breasts, return to a boil, cover, lower heat and simmer until the chicken is cooked all the way through but not overdone. Approximately 30 minutes. Remove the chicken and place in a bowl to cool; reserving broth.

Bring broth to a boil; add all the vegetables except half the parsley and the noodles. Simmer the vegetables covered until they begin to soften. Add the noodles and continue to simmer until the noodles are soft, about 7 minutes; stirring the soup occasionally. Meanwhile remove the skin from the chicken and discard. Chop the chicken into bite size pieces and set aside.

Taste the broth and adjust the seasonings to your taste. When the noodles are cooked, add the chicken pieces and the remaining parsley.

*As we have all been told—
chicken noodle soup is food
for the soul. Indulge….
it's great for your body
too…..Enjoy it with
warm, delicious
bread.*

Miso, Barley and Shitake Mushroom Soup

Bring the vegetable broth to a boil. Add barley, onion, mushrooms, cabbage, carrot, ginger and garlic. Cover and simmer until the barley is cooked and tender, 35-40 minutes.

Remove from heat and add the miso. Stir until dissolved. Add chopped cilantro.

Yield: 5 cups

2 qts. vegetable broth of your choice
⅓ cup pearled barley
1 medium onion, ¼-inch dice
1 lb. Shitake mushrooms, stems removed and sliced
2 cups green cabbage, shredded
1 carrot, peeled and shredded
2 tsp. fresh ginger, minced
4 cloves garlic, minced
4 oz. white mellow miso
1 bunch cilantro, stems removed and chopped

Chicken
Posole Revised

1½ qts. (6 cups) chicken or vegetable broth

3 boneless, skinless chicken breasts

1 medium onion, chopped

6 cloves garlic, minced

1 tsp. ground black pepper

1 tbl. chili powder

1 tsp. ground cumin

1 tsp. Mexican oregano

1 large yellow bell pepper, seeded, membranes removed and julienned

1 large red bell pepper, seeded, membranes removed and julienned

1 small chipotle pepper, chopped (available canned in Mexican foods section)

1 14-oz. can diced tomatoes

1 16-oz. can white hominy

Cilantro, chopped

Green onion chopped

Note: See end of recipe for additional ingredients as serving suggestions.

Bring the broth to a boil in a large soup pot. Add the chicken breasts and cook until they are done, about 20 minutes. Remove the chicken and set aside to cool, reserving the broth in pot.

Add the onion, garlic, seasonings and peppers to the hot broth; simmer until the vegetables are tender but not overdone. Add the tomatoes and the hominy with its liquid. Heat thoroughly.

Dice the chicken and add to the soup. Add the chopped cilantro and the green onion. Taste and adjust the seasonings to your liking. For spicier soup add more black pepper and/or chipotle pepper.

Serve with the following (optional) toppings: shredded green cabbage, finely diced radish, finely diced red onion, salsa, crumbled tortilla chips, diced fresh tomato, finely diced red, green and/or yellow pepper, cilantro, avocado and sour cream.

Curried Carrot Soup

Note: Commercial vegetable broth can be made stronger by either adding bouillon cubes to liquid broth or by doubling the recommended amounts on the package of bouillon cubes.

Heat the broth in a large soup pot. Add the onions, carrots, diced potato and curry paste. Simmer covered until the carrots are very soft. Puree soup, using a blender or food processor, until creamy and very smooth. Add half-and-half and salt to taste. If using soy creamer, add when ready to eat, making sure that the soup is not heated to a boil or the creamer will curdle.

1½ qts. strong vegetable broth (see note)
1 medium onion chopped
1 lb. carrots, peeled and sliced
1 large potato, peeled and diced
1½ tbl. Patak's mild curry paste (available at natural food stores)
1 cup half-and-half or Silk soymilk creamer
Salt to taste (taste before adding salt—commercial broth can be very salty)

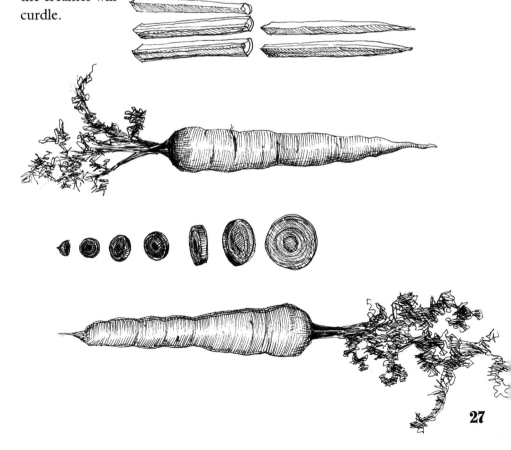

Cream of Tomato-Dill Soup

1 quart (4 cups) vegetable broth of your choice
1 large onion, peeled and chopped
1 carrot, peeled and chopped
2 cloves garlic, minced
2 28-oz. cans diced organic tomatoes, with juice
2 tbl. dill weed
2 tbl. maple syrup
Salt and pepper to taste
3 cups heavy whipping cream or Silk soymilk creamer

Heat the broth in a large soup pot. Add the onion, carrot and garlic; cook until soft. Add the tomatoes, dill and maple syrup and bring to a simmer over medium heat. Puree the contents of the soup pot in blender or food processor. Return soup to the pot, adjust the seasonings and add the cream or soy. Heat soup gently until it is warmed through.

Chill overnight for better flavor.

This makes a large batch of soup but it freezes very well.

Makes 3½ qts.

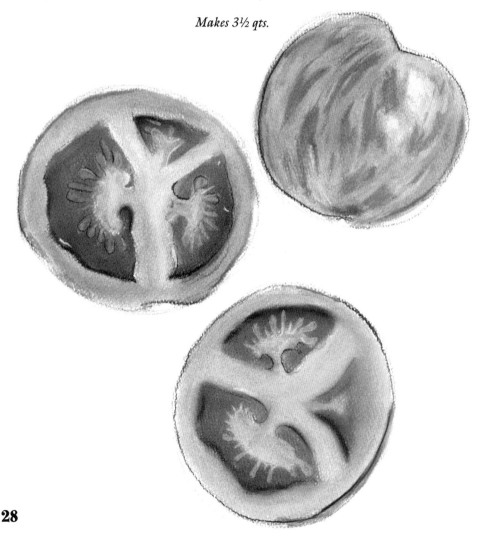

Black Bean and Roasted Butternut Squash Soup

Preheat oven to 400°.

Toss the butternut squash in the olive oil and salt. Arrange on a cookie sheet prepared with vegetable spray. Bake until tender and beginning to brown, about 30 minutes.

In large soup pot, heat the remaining 2 tbl. olive oil and sauté the chopped onion over low heat, stirring often, until light brown and caramelized; about 20 minutes.

Add the garlic, jalapeno and the tomatoes and cook for 5 minutes more. Add the beans, potatoes, broth and seasonings. Bring to a boil. The soup will create a layer of foam; skim it off as needed. Reduce the heat, cover, and simmer for 1 hour or until the beans are soft. Taste and adjust the seasonings. Add the roasted butternut squash and stir to blend.

Serve with warm tortillas, sour cream, chopped green onions, cilantro, cheese etc.

This soup is slightly laborious to make but so well worth it.

1 medium size butternut squash, peeled, seeded and cut into ½-inch cubes
2 tbl. olive oil
½ tsp. salt
Vegetable spray

2 tbl. olive oil
1 large onion, chopped
8 garlic cloves, minced or pressed
1 jalapeño, seeded and minced
1 14-oz. can crushed tomatoes
1 cup dried black beans
2 medium size russet potatoes, peeled and cubed (small)
1½ qts. vegetable broth
Salt and pepper to taste
2 tsp. ground cumin
Pinch of cayenne

moon light through oak tree
full moon
July 15, 2000

Curried Red Lentil Soup

2 qts. vegetable broth
   (homemade or store-bought)
2 cups red lentils
1 medium yellow onion, chopped
2 tbl. Patak's mild curry paste
   (available at natural food stores)
1 small bunch cilantro, stems
   removed and coarsely chopped

In large soup pot bring the broth, lentils, chopped onion and the curry paste to a boil. Lower heat, cover and simmer until the lentils are soft and fall apart, about 20-30 minutes. Remove from heat and puree, using a blender or food processor. Stir in the cilantro and serve.

Makes 1½ quarts

Saucepan

Skillet

Casserole

Stockpot

iron skillet

Cream of Broccoli Soup

Heat the broth in a large soup pot. Add the broccoli and simmer uncovered until the broccoli is soft but still bright green, stirring occasionally for even cooking.

While soup is simmering blend the flour with ⅓ cup cold water into a paste without clumps.

When broccoli is tender, puree soup using blender or food processor. Keep soup over low heat and stir in the flour/water mixture, making sure no lumps form. Season with salt and pepper. Add the cream and taste again. Adjust the seasoning if needed. Add the chopped parsley. Serve.

1½ qts. vegetable broth
1 lb. broccoli, rinsed and coarsely chopped
¼ cup flour
⅓ cup cold water
Salt and pepper to taste
1 cup cream or Silk soymilk creamer for a vegan soup
¼ cup parsley, finely chopped

Split Pea Soup (Vegan)

In a large soup pot bring the vegetable broth to a boil. Add the split peas, onion, celery, onion and bay leaf. Cover and lower heat to a simmer. Cook until peas are falling apart, about 20-25 minutes. Remove bay leaf. Puree until smooth, using blender or food processor.

Meanwhile, place the carrots and potatoes in a separate pot. Cover with water and boil until they are soft, about 10-15 minutes. Reserve their cooking liquid.

Return the puree to the soup pot, add the cooked carrots and potatoes and thin with reserved cooking liquid if soup is too thick.

Add the chopped parsley and season to taste with salt and pepper.

1 lb. dried green split peas
1½ qts. (6 cups) vegetable broth
1 medium onion, chopped
2 ribs of celery, diced
1 large bay leaf
2 carrots, diced small
2 medium sized russet potatoes, peeled and diced small
¼ cup chopped parsley

Corn and Hot Chili Chowder

1½ qts. (6 cups) strong vegetable broth (see note)

1 large onion, chopped

4 to 5 ears of corn, husked and scraped off the cob, or 3½ cups frozen corn

1 leek, sliced thin (white part only)

1 rib celery, diced

2 carrots, cut into ¼-inch dice

1 jalapeño chili, very finely chopped, including seeds

2 poblano chili, seeded and finely chopped

½ tsp. ground black pepper

1 large russet potato, peeled and cut into half-inch cubes

5 tbl. flour

½ cup water

1 pint heavy cream or Silk soymilk creamer

3 tbl. chopped parsley

3 tbl. chopped cilantro

Salt to taste

In a large soup pot heat the broth. Add the onions, corn, leeks, celery, carrots, chilies and black pepper. Return to a boil then lower heat, cover and simmer vegetables until they are tender. Add the potatoes and simmer until they soften, about 10-15 minutes.

While the soup is simmering whisk the flour and water together so no lumps remain. When the potatoes are soft, pour the flour/water mixture into the soup, stirring fast to prevent clumps from forming, but allowing the soup to thicken. Add the cream, parsley and cilantro. Add salt to taste.

Note: Commercial vegetable broth can be made stronger by either adding bouillon cubes to liquid broth or by doubling the recommended amounts on the package of bouillon cubes.

Yield: 12 cups

Tortilla Soup Bisque

Heat the broth in a large soup pot. Add the onion, garlic and jalapeño to the boiling broth and reheat to a boil. Reduce heat, cover and simmer until the onions are very tender, about 15-20 minutes. Add the salsa, canned tomatoes and seasonings, and simmer for another 15 minutes. Add the corn tortillas and simmer until they dissolve. Puree soup, using blender or food processor. Add the cream. Salt to taste.

Serve the soup accompanied with the toppings separately for everyone to add, or add the toppings yourself just before serving the soup.

Yield: 10 cups

1½ qts. (6 cups) vegetable broth
1 large onion, chopped
2 large cloves garlic, minced
1 small jalapeño pepper, seeds removed, chopped
¾ cup mild chunky salsa (such as Paul Newman's or Pace)
1 cup canned crushed tomatoes
½ tsp. oregano
½ tsp. ground cumin
½ tsp. hot chili powder

2 cups corn tortillas, torn into pieces (use your stale ones)

Salt to taste

1 cup half-and-half or Silk soymilk creamer

Garnish
Finely shredded green cabbage
Finely chopped green chilies
Diced avocado
Shredded Monterey Jack cheese
Lime wedges

Miso Soup with Sea Vegetables

2 qts. (8 cups) vegetable stock
2 cups shredded Napa cabbage
2 carrots, peeled and finely diced
1 large onion, finely chopped
8 garlic cloves, minced
2 tbl. fresh ginger, minced

1 package Soken Sea
   Vegetable salad mix
½ cup mellow miso (light
   yellow)

½ bunch cilantro, chopped
6 scallions, thinly sliced on
   the diagonal

Heat the broth in a large soup pot; add the cabbage, carrot, onion, garlic and ginger and simmer until the vegetables are tender. Add the sea vegetables and simmer for five minutes. Remove soup from heat and add the miso; stir to incorporate. In order to preserve the beneficial nutrients provided by the miso do not boil again.

Serve with chopped cilantro and scallion.

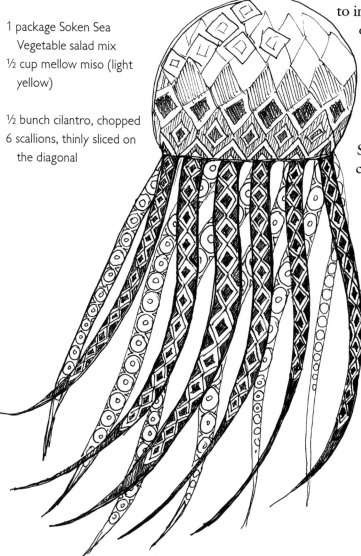

Velvety Sweet Potato and Roasted Yellow Pepper Cream Soup

In a large soup pot, boil the yams and the peppers in the broth until they are very soft and break apart (about 20 minutes). Puree soup, using blender or food processor.

Season with salt and pepper. Add the cream or Silk creamer.

Serve hot, garnished with the parsley, red bell pepper and onion.

1 qt. (4 cups) vegetable broth
1 lb. Jewel yams (about 2 medium), peeled and diced
2 canned roasted yellow peppers, diced
Salt and pepper to taste
1 cup half-and-half, or Silk soymilk creamer for a vegan soup

Garnish
Finely chopped parsley
1 red bell pepper seeded, membranes removed and very finely chopped
1 small red onion, very finely diced

potatoes
Red — 85¢/lb
Bakers & yellow 70¢/lb
all organic

organic
Onions
2 LBS/2.00 !!

Lentil Potato Soup

1½ qts. (6 cups) vegetable broth, homemade or commercial

½ lb. French green lentils, rinsed

1 large onion, diced small
2 ribs celery, diced small
2 large carrots, diced small
2 cloves garlic, minced
1 tbl. olive oil
1 tsp. sea salt
1 tsp. black pepper

2 large russet potatoes, peeled and cubed small
2 small fresh ripe tomatoes, crushed in a food processor

¼ cup parsley, chopped
Grated cheese

Bring vegetable broth to a boil in a large soup pot.

Add the lentils, onion, celery, carrots, garlic, olive oil, salt and pepper. Return to a boil, then cover, lower heat and simmer for 20 minutes. Add the potatoes and the tomatoes. Simmer until lentils and potatoes are soft, about 10 minutes. Remove from heat, adjust seasoning and add the chopped parsley.

Serve with grated cheese for a delicious lunch.

THE DIVAN PARISIEN RESTAURANT

Tuscan White Bean Soup

2 qts. (8 cups) vegetable broth of your choice (see note)

12-oz. dried cannellini beans

1 medium onion, chopped

10 garlic cloves, minced

2 tsp. fresh rosemary, chopped small

3 ribs celery, diced very small

2 tbl. olive oil

1 tsp. salt

2 tsp. black pepper

½ cup chopped parsley

2 tbl. balsamic vinegar

Shaved Parmesan or Romano cheese

In a large soup pot, heat the vegetable broth. Add the cannellini beans, chopped onion, minced garlic, rosemary, diced celery and olive oil. Bring to a boil, cover and simmer about 1-1½ hours, until the beans are very tender and start to fall apart. This will thicken the soup. Season with salt and pepper. Just before serving, add the parsley and the balsamic vinegar. Serve with Parmesan or Romano cheese.

Note: Commercial vegetable broth can be made stronger by either adding bouillon cubes to liquid broth or by doubling the recommended amounts on the package of bouillon cubes.

"He who finds no fault in himself needs a second opinion" —Anonymous

Love Always Trusts

When we observe the world around us, it is sometimes difficult to ease into the circumstances with full knowledge that the outcome of our objective will be positive. It may well be that the final outcome is not exactly how we envisioned it to be but more often than not, beneficial to our needs for growth. This process requires trust. Proceeding with our lives in a trusting manner is challenging because the enemy of trust is Fear, a presence constantly confronting our desire and challenging our effort to trust. Putting our trust in the goodness and the power of God's love is the antidote to the wile of fear. This trust will allow us to relax and keep the door open to the flow of creativity for the everyday choices and challenges in our path, regardless of what we see with our eyes.

Naturally, this is very applicable in cooking. For instance, when trying out a new recipe, which is a little daring, maybe, because you are unfamiliar with the ingredients or the process involved, you might withdraw your decision to go ahead and fix this meal for FEAR of failure. Rid yourself of that thought and move forward with trust that you are capable—cook your heart out. The promise is that something soulful will be served, and just maybe you will have invented a new recipe. How delicious is that?

Anne

"...and I've long believed that good food, good eating, is all about risk"

—Anthony Bourdain

Salads

"Cooking is at once child's play
and adult joy.
And cooking done with care
is an act of love."
—Craig Claiborne

Harvest Rice

Preheat oven to 350°

Cook rice in 3 cups of water until it is absorbed, about 45 minutes. Transfer to bowl, fluff with a fork and let cool.

Meanwhile, toss diced butternut squash with oil and place on a greased baking sheet. Roast until soft and browned, about 30 to 40 minutes. Add squash to rice.

Add all the vegetables, the cranberries and the nuts to the rice. Mix lightly.

Whisk the oil, vinegar, honey, salt, sage and pepper until well blended, pour over the salad and toss.

Makes 2-2 ½ quarts

1 ½ cups brown and wild rice blend (a premixed blend available at natural food stores)

1 lb. butternut squash, peeled, seeded and diced

2 tbl. olive oil

1 small red bell pepper, seeded and diced

1 small purple onion, chopped fine

3 celery ribs, diced

2 green onions, sliced

½ cup dried cranberries

Small bunch fresh parsley, chopped fine

1 cup pecans, halved

Dressing

½ cup olive oil

⅓ cup apple cider vinegar

2 tbl. honey

½ tsp. salt

1 tsp. rubbed sage

½ tsp. black pepper

43

Baby Lima Bean and Garlic Salad

1 cup dried baby lima beans
plus 2 cups water for a
white bean salad,
or
3 cups frozen baby lima beans,
thawed, for a light green
bean salad

½ large or 1 small red onion,
finely diced
¼ cup Italian parsley, finely
chopped

Dressing
5 tbl. olive oil
¼ cup red wine vinegar
6 cloves garlic, crushed
Salt to taste
1 tsp. ground black pepper

Place lima beans and water in 3 qt.
pot fitted with lid. Bring
water and beans to a boil,
lower heat, cover with lid
and simmer until water
is absorbed, about 40
minutes. Pour beans into
a colander and rinse with
cold water. Transfer to
mixing bowl.

Add onion and
parsley to beans in
bowl.

Whisk all dressing
ingredients
together; pour
over beans and
vegetables. Toss.

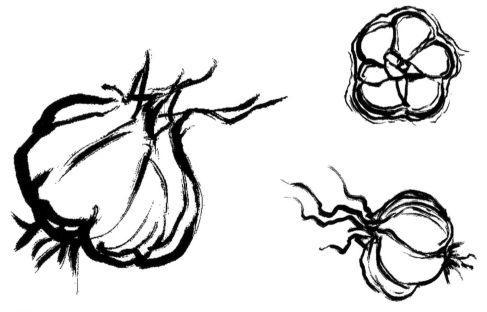

Indonesian Brown Rice and Cashew Salad

Cook the rice with the water until water is absorbed, about 30-35 minutes. Transfer to large mixing bowl and cool.

While rice is cooking, prepare the vegetables; add to cooled rice. Add the cashews.

Whisk dressing ingredients in a small bowl and pour over the salad. Toss gently until well incorporated. Best eaten at room temperature.

Papaya concentrate is available only in 32 oz. bottles. The remainder can be used in smoothies, as a sweetener in other dressings, mixed with yogurt, as fruit salad topping, ice cream topping etc…

1 cup brown basmati rice
2 cups water

3 celery ribs, sliced thin on the diagonal
4 green onions, sliced on the diagonal
1 red bell pepper, seeded, membranes removed and sliced a fine julienne
1 cup bean sprouts
1 cup chopped cilantro
1 cup roasted, salted cashews

Dressing
½ cup vegetable oil
¼ cup tamari
½ cup papaya concentrate
¼ cup brown rice vinegar
¼ cup orange juice
4 garlic cloves, minced or pressed

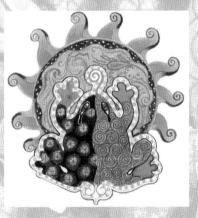

Chicken Picatta Pasta Salad

Preheat oven to 350°

½ lb. pasta pennini

3 boneless, skinless chicken breast halves

Place all marinade ingredients in a blender jar; mix well until the rosemary is pulverized.

Place the chicken in a bowl and cover with marinade. Let sit for 10 minutes, then place the chicken on a greased baking pan or cookie sheet. Pour the remaining marinade over chicken and roast for 25-30 minutes or until juices run clear when chicken is pierced with a fork. Cool and dice into bite-sized pieces.

Marinade

Juice of 1 lemon

½ tsp. salt

½ tsp. ground black pepper

2 tbl. olive oil

1 tsp. rosemary

Vegetable spray

⅓ cup small capers (non-pareilles)

1 or 2 roasted red bell peppers (canned or jarred)

2 tbl. chopped parsley

While chicken is roasting, cook the pasta in 2-3 qts of boiling salted water. Drain, rinse in cold water, and place in large mixing bowl. Add the capers, red bell pepper, parsley, and diced chicken.

Dressing

⅔ cup olive oil

½ cup fresh squeezed lemon juice

1 tsp. salt

1 tsp. ground black pepper

2 tsp. rosemary

Make the dressing in a blender, making sure the rosemary is again well chopped. Add to the pasta salad and toss. Adjust the seasonings to your liking. Mix well and serve.

Couscous and Roasted Eggplant Salad

Preheat oven to 400°

Place couscous in large mixing bowl and cover just barely with boiling water. Let stand until the water has been absorbed, about 5 minutes. Fluff with a fork and break up all clumps.

Toss sliced eggplant in olive oil and salt. Spray a baking sheet with vegetable spray and arrange the sliced eggplant cut side up on the sheet. Bake for 20 minutes, or until dark brown. Add to the couscous with the green onions.

Combine all dressing ingredients in blender, mix until a smooth liquid forms. Add to the couscous and eggplant and toss well.

Makes 4 to 5 cups

1 12-oz. box couscous (various brands available at natural food stores) or 2 cups dry couscous
Boiling water

3 Japanese eggplants sliced into ¾-inch rounds
¼ cup olive oil
½ tsp. salt
3 green onions, sliced

Vegetable spray for baking sheet

Dressing
½ cup olive oil
2 cloves garlic, pressed or minced
1 tsp. salt
1 tsp. cumin
1 cup chopped cilantro
¼ cup apple cider vinegar

Hula Salad

1½ cups dried black-eyed peas
(4 cups frozen black-eyed peas
may be used—they do not
require cooking, but need to be
thawed)
3 cups water

½ small, well-ripened, pineapple,
peeled, cored and cubed
1 small red bell pepper, seeded,
membranes removed and diced
1 small red onion, diced fine
2 green onions, chopped
1 small jalapeño, seeded and
minced
1 cup coarsely chopped cilantro

Dressing
½ cup vegetable oil
½ cup papaya
concentrate
5 tbl. fresh squeezed
lemon juice
3 cloves garlic, minced
or pressed
1 tsp. salt
1 tsp. chili
powder

Cook the black-eyed peas in the water,
covered, until all the water is absorbed,
30-60 minutes. If the peas are still a little
crunchy, add ¼ cup hot water to the pot
and continue cooking until water is again
absorbed. Make sure peas remain covered
during cooking time. Drain, rinse and
transfer to a large mixing bowl.

While peas are cooking, prepare the
pineapple and the remaining vegetables. Add
to the peas.

Whisk dressing ingredients in a small bowl,
add to the salad and toss. Great summer
salad!

Tofu-Olive Salad

2 cakes (packages) of extra firm tofu,
drained, pressed dry (place in colander
with a weight such as a dinner plate on
top) and diced into ½-inch cubes
1 very large or 2 medium size red bell
peppers, seeded, membranes removed
and cut in a very thin julienne
2 3-oz. cans sliced black olives, drained
1 bunch green onion, chopped (include
most of the green)
½ cup chopped parsley
2 tsp. oregano

Dressing
⅓ cup olive oil
¼ cup whole grain Dijon mustard
¼ cup fresh lemon juice
1 tsp. salt

Toss tofu, red bell peppers, olives, green onion, parsley
and oregano in a large bowl.

Whisk dressing ingredients in a small bowl and pour
over the tofu mixture. Toss and serve. Keeps well for
several days.

Udon Noodle Salad
with Shitake Mushrooms and Coconut Milk

1 package (8.8-oz.) brown rice
    Udon noodles
Boiling water

8 oz. Shitake mushrooms
1 tbl. butter or olive oil
1 small white onion
3 oz. fresh ginger, peeled and cut
    in a very fine julienne

4 green onions, sliced
½ cup cilantro, chopped

Dressing
¼ cup canola oil
2 tbl. toasted sesame oil
1½ cups coconut milk
Rind of 2 limes (green part only)
Juice of 2 limes
Juice of 2 lemons
1 tbl. fresh ginger, peeled and
    minced
2 garlic cloves, minced or pressed
1 tsp. salt

Break Udon noodles in half and cook in a large pot of boiling salted water until tender but still firm. Drain and rinse in cold water. Place in a large mixing bowl and set aside.

Clean mushrooms by cutting off the tough part of the stem. Slice.

Heat the butter or oil in a large frying pan, add the onion and ginger. Sauté until onion is transparent and starts to brown. Add the mushrooms and cook, stirring occasionally until they are tender, 5 to 10 minutes. Transfer to large mixing bowl, add the noodles, and green onion and cilantro.

Place all dressing ingredients in a blender jar and blend on low speed until uniform. Pour dressing over the noodles and toss. Adjust seasonings to your liking.

Tuscan Rotelli Pasta

½ lb. rainbow or plain rotelli pasta, cooked in 4 quarts salted water, drained and rinsed in cold water; set aside in large mixing bowl

Preheat oven to 375°

Toss sliced eggplant in a little olive oil to coat each side. Place on greased cookie sheet and bake until well browned, about 45 minutes. Add to cooked pasta.

Place the pinenuts in a pie pan or baking sheet, place in the overn and toast golden, about 10 minutes.

Add all the vegetables to the cooked pasta and toss.

Whisk all dressing ingredients in a small bowl until well blended. Adjust the seasonings to your liking and toss with the pasta.

2 Japanese eggplants, sliced into 1-inch rounds
Olive oil
¼ cup pinenuts, toasted
2 roasted red peppers, canned or fresh, sliced into thin strips
2 green onions, sliced
2 oz. sundried tomatoes, reconstituted sliced julienne
1 6-oz. jar whole artichoke hearts, drained and quartered
¼ cup Kalamata olives, pitted and halved
¼ cup parsley, chopped
2 sprigs fresh basil, sliced thin

Dressing
½ cup extra virgin olive oil
1 tbl. honey
¼ cup red wine vinegar
1 tsp. salt
1 tsp. fennel seed

~ This salad is SOOO good - it's got something for everyone!

Blackened Chicken Salad

6 boneless chicken breast halves
with skin on
Blackening spice (see recipe
page 177)

2 sweet apples cored, quartered
and sliced ultra thin cross wise
Juice of one lemon
Juice of one lime
Zest of one lemon
Zest of one lime

1 red bell pepper seeded,
membranes removed and cut
julienne
1 yellow bell pepper seeded,
membranes removed and cut
julienne
1 small bunch green onions, sliced
(green and white parts)
¼ cup cilantro, chopped
4 ribs celery, diced fine

Dressing
1½ cups Vegenaise
2 tsp. blackening spice
1 tsp. fructose

Preheat oven to 350°

Prepare a baking pan with vegetable spray.

Place chicken breasts in baking pan and cover generously with blackening spice. Bake for 25 to 30 minutes, until no longer pink in middle. Allow to cool, remove skin and dice.

While chicken is baking, prepare the apples and drench with lemon and lime juices. Add the zests, bell peppers, chopped green onions, cilantro and celery.

Whisk all dressing ingredients together.

Add cooled diced chicken to apple mixture and toss with the dressing.

Secret Salad

1 cup short grain brown rice
2 cups water

1 package soy tempeh, cut into
⅟₂-inch cubes
Oil for frying
1 15-oz. can adzuki beans drained
and well rinsed (or 2 cups
cooked dried adzuki beans)
1 cup Kalamata olives, pitted and
coarsely chopped
1 6-oz. jar artichoke hearts, plain
or marinated, thinly sliced
¾ cup green onions, sliced
½ cup parsley, chopped

Dressing
¼ cup fresh lemon juice
½ cup olive oil
2 tbl. red wine vinegar
1 tsp. dried oregano
3 garlic cloves, crushed
½ tsp. salt

Rinse rice under cold water. Place 2 cups water in pot and bring to a boil. Add rice to water and bring to a boil again; reduce heat and cook rice until water is absorbed, about 30 minutes. Transfer to mixing bowl, fluff with a fork to separate grains, and cool.

Sauté cubed tempeh in a little oil (adding some as needed) until toasted and golden brown. Toss for even browning. Add to rice.

Add drained beans to cooled rice.

Add olives, artichoke hearts, green onions and parsley to beans and rice.

Whisk all dressing ingredients well, add to salad and toss.

Caravan Couscous Salad

2 cups couscous
Boiling water to cover
⅔ cup golden raisins
  (Thompson seedless
  may be used)

Place couscous in a large mixing bowl and add enough boiling water to just cover. Allow to stand until water has been absorbed, about 5 minutes. Fluff with a fork, toss in the raisins and allow to cool.

1 cup green onion, sliced
¾ cup shredded carrots
½ cup cilantro, chopped
1 15-oz. can garbanzo beans,
  drained and rinsed

Prepare the onion, carrots and cilantro. Add to the couscous. Add the garbanzo beans.

Place all dressing ingredients in a blender, mix on high speed. Pour over salad and mix well.

Dressing
½ cup roasted red peppers
  (canned or in a jar)
4 garlic cloves
1 tsp. salt
¾ cup olive oil
½ cup red wine vinegar
1 tbl. crushed red chilies

Asian Vegetable Salad

1 cup carrots, shredded

3 cups bok choy, thinly sliced across the vein

3 cups Napa cabbage, thinly sliced across the vein

4 oz. shitake mushrooms, stems removed and thinly sliced

4 oz. snow peas, strings removed

2 oz. daikon sprouts (or green sprouts)

2 oz. mung bean sprouts

1 medium red bell pepper, julienne

½ cup water chestnuts, sliced

Crispy Chinese noodles (optional)

Dressing

3 cloves garlic, minced or pressed

1 cup Vegenaise

3 tbl. tamari or soy sauce

3 tbl. dijon mustard

1 tbl. olive oil

1 tsp. crushed red pepper flakes

Place the prepared vegetables in a large bowl and mix them together.

Whisk the dressing ingredients together until well blended. Pour over the vegetables and toss. Transfer to serving bowl and top with the crispy noodles just before serving.

Rosebud Potato Salad (Vegan)

2 lbs. baby or small red potatoes, unpeeled
1 small purple onion, finely chopped
4 celery ribs, finely diced
½ cup fresh parsley, chopped
¼ cup brown rice vinegar
1 tsp. salt
1 tsp. ground black pepper
1 cup Vegenaise

Wash the potatoes well, then boil them in a large pot of salted water until tender when pierced with a fork, about 30 minutes. Drain and let them cool just enough to handle. Quarter potatoes into large mixing bowl and toss with vinegar and salt while still warm.

Toss the vegetables with the potatoes. Add the Vegenaise, black pepper and mix. Refrigerate until ready to eat.

Serves 6

Macaroni Salad (Vegan)

2 cups elbow pasta, cooked and rinsed in cold water
4 ribs celery, finely diced
1 4-oz. can roasted red pepper, diced
1 cup sliced black olives
4 green onions, sliced
½ small red onion, finely diced
⅔ cup Cascadian Farms sweet pickle relish (available in natural food stores)
2 cups Vegenaise
2 tsp. black pepper
1 tsp. salt

Place first seven ingredients in a large salad bowl. Add the Vegenaise, pepper and salt and mix lightly. Taste and adjust seasonings to your liking.

Make salad one day ahead for best flavor.

56

Saffron Basmati Rice Salad

2 cups white basmati rice
3½ cups water
½ tsp. saffron threads

2 small bunches green onions,
  sliced
1 cup finely diced red bell pepper
1 cup finely diced celery
1 English cucumber, seeded and
  finely diced
½ cup finely chopped red onion
½ cup Major Grey's mango
  chutney

Dressing
⅓ cup vegetable oil
2 garlic cloves, pressed
1 tbl. Patak's mild curry paste
  (available in natural food stores)
1 tsp. salt
⅓ cup honey or maple syrup
⅓ cup apple cider vinegar

Place rice, water and saffron in 3 quart pot and bring water to a boil. Reduce heat to low, cover and simmer for 18 to 20 minutes, until all the water has been absorbed.

Transfer to large mixing bowl, fluff and cool.

While rice is cooking, prepare the vegetables. Add to the cooled rice. Add the mango chutney and toss.

Whisk dressing ingredients in a small bowl and pour over the salad, toss gently again.

Roasted Yam Salad

3 lbs. red-skinned yams
¼ cup olive oil
Vegetable spray

1 large red onion, thinly sliced
¼ cup chopped parsley

Dressing
⅓ cup olive oil
2 tbl. Dijon mustard
¼ cup honey
¼ cup apple cider vinegar
1 tsp. salt

Preheat oven to 375°

Prepare a baking pan with vegetable spray.

Peel yams and dice into 1½-inch cubes. Toss with ¼-cup olive oil. Place on prepared baking sheet and roast until soft, about 35-40 minutes. Transfer to a mixing bowl and cool.

Add onion and parsley to the yams.

Whisk dressing ingredients vigorously in a bowl. Add to the yams and toss.

Serves 4 to 6

Chow Mein Noodle Salad

Place cooled noodles in a large mixing bowl.

Toss in prepared vegetables, water chestnuts, bean sprouts, seeds and nuts.

Whisk dressing ingredients in a small bowl and pour over the salad, toss to blend.

1 8 18-oz. package Annie Chun's Chow Mein noodles cooked, rinsed and cooled (available at specialty stores and natural food stores)

3 cups shredded Napa cabbage
1 cup shredded carrots
1 bunch green onions, thinly sliced on a slant, white part included
1 can sliced water chestnuts, drained
2 oz. bean sprouts
¾ cup toasted almonds, chopped
¾ cup tamari sunflower seeds (available at natural food stores)
1 tbl. black sesame seeds (regular may be used, but toasted)

Dressing
¾ cup brown rice vinegar
⅓ cup turbinado sugar
⅓ cup vegetable oil
¼ cup honey
⅓ cup tamari
1 tsp. Chinese five spice blend (available at most stores)

59

Temple Tofu

2 lbs. extra firm tofu,
drained and pressed dry with paper towels

2 ribs celery, finely diced
1 small red bell pepper, finely diced
3 green onions, sliced
1 cup roasted, salted cashews
½ cup unsweetened coconut (wide flake is preferred)
½ cup chopped dried mango (use scissors to cut)

Dressing
2 cups Vegenaise
1 cup Major Grey's mango chutney
3 tbl. fresh squeezed lemon juice

Cube the tofu into ½-inch chunks and place in a large mixing bowl.

Add the celery, red bell pepper, green onion, cashews, coconut,
dried mango and toss.

Whisk dressing ingredients together and pour over the
salad, toss to blend.

Curried Chicken Salad
with Grapes and Mango Chutney

Preheat oven to 350°

Place chicken, skin side up, on slightly oiled baking sheet. Rub a tiny bit of oil on skin and season with salt and pepper. Roast about 20 minutes, or until done.

Remove chicken from pan, cool and remove skin. Chop into ½-inch cubes and place in mixing bowl. Add grapes, celery, green onion and cilantro to chicken.

Whisk all dressing ingredients together and pour over chicken mixture; toss to blend.

4 boneless chicken breasts, skin on
Olive oil
Salt and pepper to taste
2 cups red seedless grapes, halved
2 ribs celery, diced fine
½ cup cilantro, chopped fine
¾ cup green onions, chopped

Dressing
1 cup Vegenaise
1 cup Major Grey's mango chutney
1 tbl. Patak's mild curry paste (available in natural food stores or ethnic markets)
1 tbl. lemon juice

Dilled Pea Salad

Place the peas in a mixing bowl.

Add the onion, parsley and dill.

Whisk all dressing ingredients together and pour over the peas. Toss. For a sweeter salad add more honey.

3 cups fresh or frozen peas, thawed, (if using fresh, blanch in rapidly boiling water until they turn bright green)
1 small red onion, finely chopped
¼ cup chopped parsley
1 tsp. dill weed

Dressing
¼ cup honey
⅓ cup vegetable oil
¼ cup red wine vinegar
1 tsp. dill weed
½ tsp. salt

61

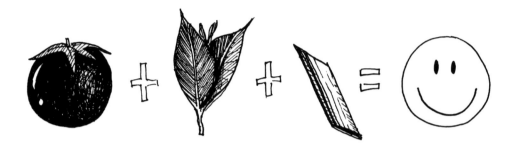

Penne with Summer Tomatoes, Basil and Garlic

½ lb. penne or pennini pasta
cooked in salted water, rinsed in
cold water and set aside in large
mixing bowl
6-8 small to medium Heirloom or
sun-ripened tomatoes, halved,
seeded and cut julienne or thinly
sliced lengthwise
½ bunch fresh basil, stems
removed and sliced thin
(chiffonade)
4 cloves garlic, pressed
1 tsp. crushed red chilies
1 tsp. sea salt
3 tbl. good quality olive oil

Mix together the cooked pasta, julienne tomatoes and sliced basil. Press the garlic into the pasta. Add the chilies, olive oil and salt. Toss.

Makes 4 to 6 servings

Broccoli, Mushroom and Roasted Red Pepper Salad

Place the broccoli, mushrooms, red pepper and basil in a large mixing bowl; toss.

Whisk dressing ingredients together, pour over the vegetables and toss.

1 large broccoli crown cut into florets

3 cups very fresh white mushrooms, sliced

1 large canned roasted red pepper, cut julienne style

½ cup fresh basil chiffonade (sliced very thin)

Dressing
½ cup olive oil
¼ cup umeboshi vinegar (Japanese plum vinegar)
¼ cup fresh squeezed lemon juice

Mean Green Bean Salad

2 lb. young green beans (blue lakes) or Haricots Verts
1 small purple onion, sliced very thin
½ cup fresh parsley, chopped fine

Dressing
½ cup quality olive oil
⅓ cup red wine vinegar .
3 garlic cloves, pressed or minced
Salt and pepper to taste

Snip the stem from the green beans with scissors. Wash.

Either steam the beans or cook them in lots of boiling water until they turn bright green and just become tender. Drain and rinse them in cold water to stop them from cooking further. Set aside.

Add onion and parsley to the well-drained beans.

Whisk dressing ingredients together, pour over the beans, toss to coat well. Taste to adjust to your liking.

Remember! it only takes a few minutes to turn greenbeans bright green — don't over cook!!

Greek Garbo Salad

Place drained garbanzo beans in a large mixing bowl. Add the vegetables, olives and crumbled feta cheese to the salad.

Whisk dressing ingredients together and pour over the salad; toss lightly to avoid mashing the feta cheese.

Can be made a day ahead.

2 15-oz. cans garbanzo beans, drained and rinsed

1 large red bell pepper, seeded, membranes removed and sliced in a fine julienne

4 green onions, sliced (white and green parts)

½ small red onion, diced

4 parsley sprigs, coarsely chopped

1 cup California sliced black olives

4 oz. feta cheese, coarsely crumbled

Dressing

½ cup olive oil

⅓ cup red wine vinegar

1 tsp. salt

4 cloves of garlic, minced or pressed

½ tsp. oregano

½ tsp. ground black pepper

Fiesta Salad

1 15-oz. can pinto beans, drained and rinsed

1 15-oz. can red beans, drained and rinsed

1 small jicama, peeled and diced

1 basket cherry tomatoes, halved

1 bunch red radishes, thinly sliced

1 red bell pepper, seeded and finely diced

1 yellow bell pepper, seeded and finely diced

1 jalapeno, seeded and finely diced

1 cup frozen or fresh corn

1 cup green onion, sliced

1 small red onion, finely diced

1 small bunch cilantro, coarsely chopped

Dressing

½ cup vegetable oil

2 tbl. honey

½ cup red wine vinegar

salt to taste

1 tsp. dried oregano

Place all salad ingredients in large mixing bowl.

Whisk dressing ingredients together and pour over the bean/vegetable mixture, toss gently.

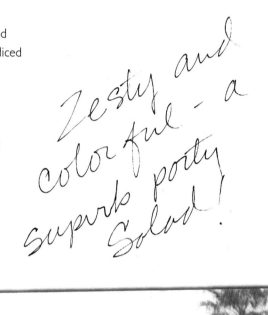

Zesty and colorful – a superb party salad!

Roasted Beet
and Baby Spinach Salad

Preheat oven to 375°

Scrub unpeeled whole beets. Place them
on a baking sheet prepared with parchment
paper to avoid difficult cleaning. Roast
whole until they feel soft to pressure. The
roasting time will vary as beet size varies
greatly (small beets take about 1 hour).
Remove from oven and cool. When cooled
enough so they can be handled, peel them
and cut into chunks about 1½-inches in size
and place them in a mixing bowl. Toss them
with the olive oil and black pepper. Place
them again, in a single layer, on a baking
sheet with new parchment paper and roast
for 15 to 20 minutes longer to caramelize
them. Meanwhile, make the dressing by
whisking syrup, vinegar and salt together.

Transfer beets to a large mixing bowl, add
the corn and all dressing ingredients, toss
well and add the spinach. Toss again.

3 lb. pounds red or golden beets
¼ cup olive oil
1 tsp. ground black pepper
½ cup fresh or frozen corn
2 cups very fresh baby spinach
(1 5 5-oz. bag) washed

Dressing
½ cup maple syrup
¼ cup brown rice vinegar
½ tsp. salt (may be omitted)

*Unbelievable!
Rich and
Shimmering -
Jewel-Like reds
contrast with
blast of green. shiny*

Love is Patient

In a world of immediate satisfaction, the proverbial "Patience is a Virtue" is hardly fostered.

Let us consider Patience . . . We learn extensively about ourselves while waiting for what we desire. An abundance of emotions may arise, from frustration, anger, doubt, or intolerance, to possibly giving up altogether and foregoing the opportunity to master perseverance and attain the fullness of the desired goal. The gift rewarded by patience exceeds the smallness of our imagination. However large or small the object of our desire may be, we ought to love it enough to be willing to wait the entire time it takes to become its worthy recipient.

This is also true of cooking. The most nourishing foods, the most delicious dishes, and most loved meals take time to prepare. Food prepared with patience is not necessarily an intricate ordeal. Simple dishes require less cooking time, but it is our attitude while creating the dish that requests patience.

Adding a touch of love and care instead of throwing together individual ingredients will make all the difference. Approach cooking as you would an offering; as a time of reflection, of prayer, or of paying honor to the wellness of the body—yours and your loved ones with whom you will share your table.

Anne

Tomato, Cucumber and Green Olive Salad

12 ripe but firm Roma tomatoes, sliced thin

2 English or hothouse cucumbers, sliced thin

1 large white onion, peeled, cut in half and sliced paper thin

1 6-oz. can green olives (preferably Santa Barbara Olive Co. brand), halved

½ cup chopped Italian parsley

Dressing

1 cup olive oil

½ cup red wine vinegar

8 garlic cloves, pressed or minced

1½ tsp. salt

Toss vegetables in a large mixing bowl. Whisk dressing ingredients until well blended and add to the vegetables. Toss and chill.

Tropical Carrot Salad

Place all salad ingredients in a large mixing bowl.

Whisk dressing ingredients together and pour over the salad, toss and chill.

Refreshing on a hot summer day. Great for barbecues.

8 dried apricots, rehydrated (place in a little boiling water and let stand 10 minutes), diced

3 cups shredded carrots (about 4 to 5 large carrots)

1 8-oz. can crushed pineapple (unsweetened) with liquid

½ cup coconut flakes (unsweetened)

2 green onions, white and green parts, sliced

½ cup chopped cilantro

Dressing

¾ cup Vegenaise

½ cup papaya concentrate

Juice of one lemon

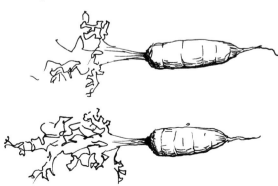

The Big Easy Salad

2 cups Lundberg Wildblend rice (a
blend of wild and brown rices,
available at natural food stores)
4 cups water
2 cups frozen peas
1 cup frozen shelled Edamame
beans
½ cup pinenuts, toasted
1 small red onion, finely chopped
2 green onions, sliced
1 red bell pepper, seeded,
membranes removed, diced
¼ cup chopped parsley (preferably
Italian)

Dressing
¾ cup olive oil
½ cup red wine vinegar
7 garlic cloves, minced or pressed
1 tbl. blackening spice (see recipe
page 177)
1 tsp. salt

Place rice and water in 3 quart pot and bring water to a boil. Reduce heat to low, cover and simmer for 25-30 minutes, until all the water has been absorbed.

Transfer to mixing bowl, fluff and add frozen peas and beans. The warm rice will thaw them and help chill the rice.

While rice is cooking, toast the pinenuts in a preheated oven at 400° until they turn golden brown. Add to the cooled rice.

Add red onion, green onion, red bell pepper and parsley to the rice.

Whisk the dressing ingredients together and pour over the salad. Toss.

Seven Veil Chicken Salad

Preheat oven to 350°

Place the chicken breasts on a sprayed baking pan or cookie sheet. Sprinkle chicken generously with blackening spice and roast for 25 to 30 minutes, depending on the size of the chicken breasts. Cool chicken, remove the skin and dice into bite-sized cubes. Transfer chicken to a large mixing bowl and add the dates, pistachios, red onion, green onion, zucchini and cilantro.

Whisk dressing ingredients together and pour over the chicken mixture; toss. Best flavor when eaten immediately but also delicious cold after refrigeration.

Remaining curry paste may be used as curry powder in any of your favorite curry dishes.

6 boneless chicken breast halves with skin on
Blackening Spice for sprinkling (see recipe page 177)
Vegetable spray

1½ cups chopped dates
1 cup pistachios, coarsely chopped (¾ lbs. in-shell yields 1 cup shelled)
1 small red onion, diced small
4 green onions, chopped
2 large or 4 small zucchini, diced
¾ cup chopped cilantro

Dressing
⅔ cup Major Grey's mango chutney
½ cup olive oil
⅓ cup red wine vinegar
1 tbl. Patak's mild curry paste (available at natural food stores or ethnic markets)
½ tsp. salt
4 garlic cloves, minced or pressed

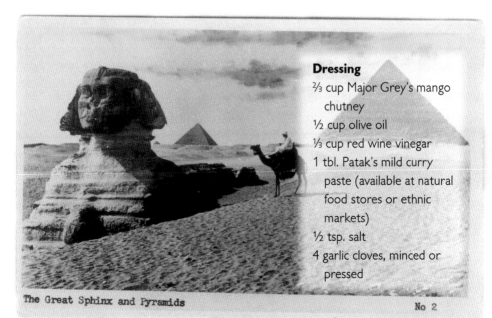

The Great Sphinx and Pyramids

No 2

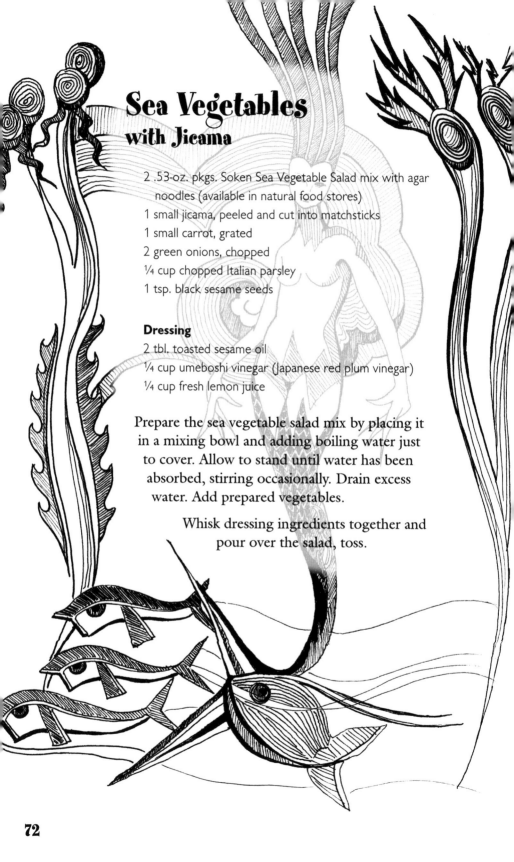

Sea Vegetables
with Jicama

2 .53-oz. pkgs. Soken Sea Vegetable Salad mix with agar
  noodles (available in natural food stores)
1 small jicama, peeled and cut into matchsticks
1 small carrot, grated
2 green onions, chopped
¼ cup chopped Italian parsley
1 tsp. black sesame seeds

Dressing
2 tbl. toasted sesame oil
¼ cup umeboshi vinegar (Japanese red plum vinegar)
¼ cup fresh lemon juice

Prepare the sea vegetable salad mix by placing it
in a mixing bowl and adding boiling water just
to cover. Allow to stand until water has been
absorbed, stirring occasionally. Drain excess
water. Add prepared vegetables.

Whisk dressing ingredients together and
pour over the salad, toss.

Southwestern Brown Rice Salad
with Black Beans and Tempeh

Cook rice in water until completely absorbed, about 30-35 minutes. Transfer to mixing bowl, fluff and allow to cool.

Dice the tempeh into ½-inch cubes. Fry in hot oil over medium heat until golden brown. Transfer onto paper towels to absorb excess oil. Add to rice.

If using fresh corn, scrape kernels off the cob into the rice/ tempeh mixture. If using frozen corn, add the frozen corn to the salad (it will help cool the salad and defrost the kernels). Add beans, green onions, red onion and cilantro.

Whisk dressing ingredients together and pour over the salad, toss.

This salad is best when made a day ahead.

Dressing
⅓ cup canola oil
2 tsp. chili powder
1 tsp. salt
3 cloves garlic, minced or pressed
3 tbl. cider vinegar or rice vinegar

1 cup brown basmati rice
2 cups water

8 oz. Five Grain (or any flavor) tempeh
Vegetable oil for frying
1 cup fresh or frozen corn
1 cup cooked black beans (canned or dried)
4 green onions, sliced
1 small red onion, finely chopped
½ cup chopped cilantro

Sugar Snap Peas
with Sesame Seeds and Ginger Dressing

2 lbs. fresh sugar snap peas, strings removed on both sides (Select very fresh ones for more tenderness)
Boiling water

2 tbl. black or white sesame seeds, toasted
½ cup chopped cilantro

Dressing
2 oz. fresh ginger, peeled and grated (preferably juiced)
2 tbl. toasted sesame oil
1 tbl. canola oil
Juice of one lemon

Preheat oven to 400°

Fill a 4-5 qt. saucepan halfway with water and bring to a boil.

Place the sesame seeds in a pie pan or other small ovenproof dish and toast in hot oven for 10 to 15 minutes.

Drop the cleaned sugar snaps into the boiling water and blanch for 2 to 3 minutes, or just until they turn bright green. Remove promptly, drain and rinse in very cold water to retain their crispness and bright green color. Place in a large mixing bowl; add sesame seeds and cilantro.

Whisk dressing ingredients together and pour over the vegetables.

Eat soon. The sugar snaps will lose their brightness within an hour or so due to the dressing.

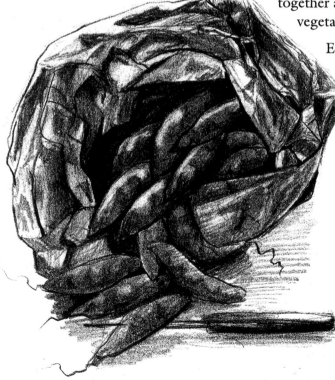

74

Chlada Felfla
Salad of Roasted Peppers with Preserved Lemons

Preheat oven
to 350°

Place prepared
peppers on oiled
baking sheet and
roast until they are
soft and dark brown,
35-40 minutes. Transfer
them to a plastic bag, let
them cool a little until they can
be handled and the skins loosen.
Promptly remove the peppers from the
bag and peel them under cold running
water.

Dice the peppers finely, transfer them to a
mixing bowl, add remaining ingredients and
toss.

Serve as a condiment or on French bread
slices as an appetizer.

2 red, 2 green, and 2 yellow bell
peppers, halved and seeded
⅓ cup olive oil
2 garlic cloves minced
2 tsp. finely diced preserved
lemon rind, page 182
2 tsp. ground cumin
Salt and pepper to taste
Fresh lemon juice to taste

Roasting the peppers is a joy — it will fill your home with the best aroma!

Moroccan Toasted Millet Salad

1 cup millet
Olive oil for frying
2 cups water
Pinch of salt

½ cup sulphured dried apricots,
   thinly sliced (unsulphured OK,
   but not as attractive)
½ cup sliced almonds
¾ cup sliced green onions
1 cup coarsely chopped cilantro,
   larger stems removed
¾ cup red bell pepper, finely diced

Dressing
½ cup olive oil
2 tbl. honey
¼ cup fresh lemon juice
½ tsp. salt
½ tsp. cumin
2 tsp. coriander
½ tsp. cinnamon
2 cloves garlic, crushed

Heat olive oil in 2 qt. cooking pot which has a lid. Add millet and toast over low heat until millet starts to brown. Stir often for even browning. Add water and salt and bring to a boil. Cover with lid, lower heat and simmer until all the water is absorbed, about 20 minutes. Transfer to mixing bowl and cool. Fluff with a fork.

Add vegetables, fruit and nuts to cooled millet.

Whisk dressing ingredients together and pour over the salad, toss.

Casablanca Carrots

Bring water to a boil in a 3-4 qt. pot. Add the carrots and cook just until the carrots are tender, 4-6 minutes. Drain, cool, and place in a mixing bowl.

Place pinenuts in a pie pan and toast until golden in a 400° oven. Add to the carrots.

Using a very small non-greased frying pan roast the cumin seeds over high heat, continually moving them to and fro. Be watchful, as they will burn quickly. When they begin to smoke, remove immediately and toss into the salad.

Add the green onion, cilantro, and olives.

Whisk dressing ingredients together and pour over the salad, toss. Best eaten at room temperature.

2 lb. carrots peeled and sliced into coins (6-8 large carrots)
⅓ cup pinenuts
1 tbl. whole cumin seed

4 green onions, sliced
1 cup chopped cilantro
½ cup Kalamata olives, pitted and halved

Dressing
¼ cup olive oil
¼ cup honey
⅓ cup red wine vinegar
1 tsp. salt

Quinoa and Olive Tabouleh

1½ cups quinoa
2½ cups water

⅔ cup green pitted olives, cut in
half (Santa Barbara Olive Co.
brand is best)
⅔ cup California sliced black olives
1 cup green onion, sliced
1½ cups finely chopped parsley
2 tsp. fresh ground black pepper

Dressing
¼ cup olive oil
¼ cup fresh squeezed lemon juice
½ tsp. salt

Place quinoa and water in a medium saucepan and bring to a boil. Cover and reduce heat to low. Cook until water has been completely absorbed. Check occasionally by inserting a knife in the center of quinoa to notice whether water at the bottom has been absorbed. Transfer to large mixing bowl and cool.

While quinoa is cooking prepare the vegetables. Add to the cooled quinoa. Add the pepper.

Whisk dressing ingredients together and pour over the salad and toss.

Greek Vegetable Salad

Quarter both tomatoes and clean out the inside parts so that nothing but the outer flesh remains. Slice them thinly and place them in a large mixing bowl.

Peel and halve the onion and slice thinly crosswise (making half moons); add to tomatoes in bowl.

Cut the cucumber lengthwise in quarters, cut out the seeds, then slice on a slant and add to tomatoes.

Add the olives.

Quarter the artichokes and add to the bowl.

Slice the red pepper julienne style and add to the vegetables in bowl.

Add the herbs and toss.

Whisk dressing ingredients together, pour over the salad and toss. Taste and adjust salt and pepper to your liking.

Using a potato peeler, shave the feta over the salad, leaving some for the top. Toss salad and place in a serving bowl. Shave the remaining cheese over top.

Best at room temperature.

Serves 8

1 beefsteak or other large summer tomato
1 large yellow or orange tomato
1 small purple onion (½ cup)
1 English cucumber
1 cup Kalamata pitted olives
1 cup canned artichokes
1 large canned roasted red pepper

½ cup chopped fresh mint
½ cup chopped fresh parsley
2 tsp. dried oregano

1 cup extra virgin olive oil
¾ cup red wine vinegar
Salt and pepper to taste
6 garlic cloves, pressed

4 oz. good quality firm feta cheese

Moondance Salad

1 8 8-oz. pkg. spelt spaghetti
(traditional spaghetti may
be used)

1 lb. extra firm tofu, well drained
and cubed into ½-inch pieces
Vegetable oil for frying

1 medium butternut squash,
peeled, seeded and cubed into
½-inch pieces
2 tbl. olive oil
Pinch of salt

1 cup canned black beans, drained
and rinsed
⅔ cup green onions chopped
⅔ parsley chopped
½ cup toasted pumpkin seeds

Dressing
¼ cup olive oil
¾ cup tamari
2 tbl. honey
¼ cup fresh lemon juice

Preheat
oven to 350°

Bring 4 quarts water to boil in large
cooking pot.

Break spaghetti into thirds, add to boiling
water and cook until soft but still a little
firm (al dente); refer to cooking directions
on package.

Transfer spaghetti to colander, drain and
rinse immediately in very cold water. Drain
well and transfer to mixing bowl.

Toss prepared butternut squash with oil
and salt until well covered. Place on lightly
oiled baking pan and roast until soft to the
touch; about 25 minutes.

While squash is roasting prepare the tofu
and fry in oil (about ½-inch deep) until
golden brown and crisp. Drain in colander
lined with paper towel to absorb all excess
oil. Add to spaghetti.

Prepare vegetables and add to spaghetti/
tofu mixture.

Add roasted squash, black beans, and
pumpkin seeds.

Whisk dressing ingredients together and
pour over the salad. Adjust seasonings to
your liking. Toss to blend.

Can I have just one more moondance with you, my love. —Van Morrison

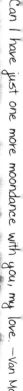

Summer Crunch

Prepare all the veggies and place in a mixing bowl.

Whisk dressing ingredients together and toss with the veggies. Taste and adjust flavor.

For a more spicy salad add more red pepper flakes. For a sweeter salad, add more apple juice concentrate.

2 regular cucumbers seeded, halved and sliced thin

OR

1 English cucumber halved and sliced thin

1 small jicama, peeled and cut into matchsticks

2 bunches radish sliced thin

1 small bunch cilantro chopped coarsely

Dressing

1 cup apple juice concentrate

2 tbl. umeboshi plum vinegar

½ tsp. crushed red pepper flakes

Juice of ½ lemon

Kung Pao Brown Rice and Tofu Salad

1½ cups short grain brown rice
3 cups water

1 lb. extra firm tofu, well drained
   and diced into ½-inch cubes
Vegetable oil for frying

1 cup toasted peanuts
⅔ cup sliced green onions (about
   1 bunch)
1 8-oz. can sliced water chestnuts
⅔ cup grated carrots

Dressing
¼ cup toasted sesame oil
½ cup tamari
¼ cup brown rice vinegar
3 cloves garlic, pressed
1 tsp. crushed red chili peppers

Cook rice and transfer to large mixing bowl to cool. Fluff rice with a fork to separate grains.

Using paper towel, pat the cubed tofu dry. Cover bottom of a frying pan with vegetable oil about ¼-inch deep and heat till hot, but not smoking. Fry the tofu till golden brown, tossing frequently for even browning. With slotted spoon transfer tofu into a strainer lined with paper towel to absorb oil. Set aside to cool.

Add peanuts, green onions, water chestnuts and carrots to rice. Add fried tofu.

Whisk dressing ingredients together. Pour over the salad and toss.

This recipe is delicious but improves overnight. It remains great for several days.

Kashmir Tofu Salad

Place all salad ingredients in a large mixing bowl and mix lightly.

Whisk dressing ingredients together. Pour over the salad and toss to coat well.

1 lb. extra firm tofu, drained, pressed dry and cubed (½-inch)

1 lb. ripe, firm summer tomatoes, seeded and cut julienne

1 small red onion, peeled, quartered and sliced ultra thin

1 5-oz. bag of pre-washed baby spinach

Dressing

½ cup vegetable oil

1 tbl. Patak's mild curry paste (available at natural food stores or ethnic markets)

2 tsp. fructose (or sugar)

⅓ cup red wine vinegar

2 garlic cloves, pressed

1 tsp. salt

83

Mediterranean Marinated Vegetables

2 large heirloom tomatoes or
  1 basket cherry tomatoes
1 6-oz. jar whole artichoke hearts,
  quartered
1 English cucumber, sliced
  lengthwise in half, then sliced
  thinly on the diagonal
1 small red onion, peeled, halved
  and sliced thinly crosswise
  (making half moons)
1 large canned roasted red pepper,
  diced
1 med. zucchini, diced
½ cup coarsely chopped Italian
  parsley

Dressing
½ cup extra virgin olive oil
⅓ cup red wine vinegar
Salt and pepper to taste
6 garlic cloves, pressed or minced

If using large tomatoes, quarter them and scrape out the seeds so that nothing remains but the outer flesh. Cherry tomatoes are halved.

In a large mixing bowl place the quartered artichoke hearts, sliced cucumber, sliced onion, prepared tomatoes, diced red pepper, diced zucchini and chopped parsley.

Whisk dressing ingredients together, pour over the vegetables and toss.

Great, refreshing and a delicious side dish or picnic salad.

Moroccan Couscous Salad

Place dry couscous in large mixing bowl and add enough boiling water to just cover the couscous. Let stand until couscous has absorbed the water, about 5 minutes. Fluff with a fork to break apart all the clumps.

Add the prepared vegetables, apricots and nuts.

Whisk dressing ingredients together until the honey has dissolved completely and pour over the salad. Adjust the seasoning to your liking. If you like it sweeter add more honey, or if you like it saltier add more salt and so on.

1½ cups couscous
Boiling water

½ cup red bell pepper, diced
½ cup purple onion, diced
½ cup green onion, thinly sliced
½ cup grated carrot
½ cup cilantro, coarsely chopped
½ cup dried apricots, sliced
   (sulfured preferably for
   appearance)
½ cup sliced almonds

Dressing
¾ cup extra virgin olive oil
½ cup red wine vinegar
1 tsp. salt
4 cloves garlic, pressed
¼ tsp. cinnamon
½ tsp. ground cumin
½ tsp. coriander
¼ tsp. ground ginger
¼ cup honey

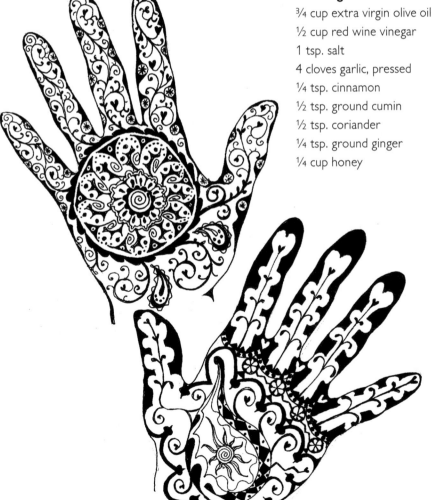

A garden of Magic
Where Joy is sung by the Meadowlark
And silence is a robe of Peace
The spirit of it a healing Potion
For the wounded heart to embrace
Soft grasses a bed of comfort
And rushing creeks humming their tunes
There love lies
Spoken forth in beauty
Revealed like fireworks
Tender as blushing spring flowers
A mountain of color
Where God mends the heart

Grass Mt.
From Green gate 3/7/99

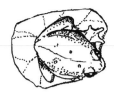
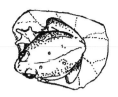

Perk-Up Salad

Peel and dice the avocados into 1-inch chunks.

Halve the cherry tomatoes.

Place the avocado, cherry tomatoes, garbanzo beans, green onion and cilantro in a mixing bowl.

Whisk dressing ingredients together, pour over the salad and gently toss.

Very, very yummy!

4 to 5 ripe but firm avocados
1 basket cherry tomatoes
1 12-oz. can garbanzo beans, drained and rinsed
3 green onions, sliced
¼ cup chopped cilantro

Dressing
1 cup papaya concentrate
Juice from 2 lemons
½ tsp. garlic powder
½ tsp. salt

Tabouleh

1½ cups bulgur wheat
1 English cucumber, quartered lengthwise and seeded
1 large tomato, quartered and seeded
2 green onions, sliced
⅔ cup chopped parsley
1 tbl. dried spearmint
2 tsp. fresh ground black pepper

Dressing
¼ cup olive oil
⅓ cup fresh squeezed lemon juice
1 tsp. salt

Place bulgur in a large mixing bowl. Pour boiling water, just enough to cover, over the bulgur. Let stand until the water has been absorbed. Fluff with a fork and cool.

Meanwhile, slice the quartered cucumber into thinner slices and then chop them across. Do the same with the tomatoes. Add to the cooled bulgur. Add the green onions, the parsley, the mint and the pepper.

Whisk dressing ingredients together and pour over the salad, toss. Adjust seasonings to taste.

Makes 1½ quarts

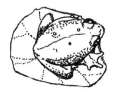

Cucumber and Feta Salad

2 English or hothouse cucumbers
1 small red onion
⅓ cup chopped fresh mint
⅓ cup chopped parsley

Dressing
⅓ cup olive oil
¼ cup red wine vinegar
4 cloves garlic, minced or pressed
1 tsp. dried oregano
1 tsp. salt

4 oz. firm feta cheese

Slice cucumbers lengthwise into quarters. Remove the seeds using the edge of a spoon or a small paring knife and slice each quarter thinly on the diagonal. Place in a large mixing bowl.

Peel and cut onion in half. Cut into very thin slices and add to the cucumbers. Add the chopped mint and parsley.

Whisk dressing ingredients together and pour over the salad. Toss well. Use a potato peeler to shave 3 ounces of the feta into the salad, toss lightly. Shave remaining feta over the top and serve.

Viva Italia Quinoa Salad

1 cup quinoa
1¾ cups water

¾ lb. ripe summer tomatoes, quartered, seeded and diced small
¾ cup chopped green onion
¼ cup chiffonade of fresh basil (sliced very fine)

Dressing
4 cloves of garlic, crushed
½ cup olive oil
2 tbl. fresh lemon juice
1 tsp. salt

Cook quinoa in 1¾ cups boiling water until all water is absorbed, about 20-30 minutes. Transfer to large mixing bowl, fluff with fork, and cool.

Prepare tomatoes, onions and basil; add to cooled quinoa.

Whisk dressing ingredients together and pour over the salad and toss.

Safari Quinoa Salad

Bring the and water quinoa to a boil, cover, and simmer until all the water has been absorbed, about 20-30 minutes. Do the same with the wild rice.

Place cooked rice and quinoa in a large mixing bowl and fluff. Allow to cool.

Add prepared vegetables and nuts to grains. Whisk dressing ingredients together. Pour over salad and toss.

Best eaten shortly after preparation as the nuts get soggy after a day or so.

1½ cups quinoa
3 cups water

½ cup wild rice
1 cup water

¾ cup shredded carrots
1 cup green onion, sliced
½ cup chopped parsley
1 cup roasted and salted cashews

Dressing
½ cup olive oil
½ cup tamari
¼ cup fresh lemon juice

A Fable

There once was a man who lived
in a fortress.
He was a simple man, a noble man.
He had suffered much.

A woman lived nearby.
The woman admired the fortress. It
stood strong and majestic.
She often dreamed about going to
see the man in the fortress.
She knew him to be of a kind heart,
of a gentle nature.
The man was handsome.

One day, the man invited her to
come inside the fortress.
So delighted, she did not consider
the dangers. She allowed herself to
be led by the man inside the fortress. The woman ignored the wisdom
of her heart.

Once inside, she knew, she would
not want to leave. The beauty she
saw and felt, captured her.

From then on, the man allowed her
inside for brief visits and then re-
quested her departure.
Each time, the woman left with great
sadness which grew larger
at each visit.
This became unbearable.
The woman could no longer remain
content and began to complain.
The beauty inside the fortress had
ensnared her.

The man saw the woman's distress
and thought it necessary to end
the visits.

The man thought it impossible for the
woman to remain inside the fortress.
He could not see room
for her.
The man knew not how to make
the beauty inside the fortress
grow larger.
The walls of the fortress were thick
and big and well established.

The woman could not understand and
lost all heart.
She begged and bargained.
She pleaded and clung.
She saw that her efforts were not
reaching inside the fortress.
The man did not hear.

The man took the woman one last
time. Then she was never to return.

Now, the woman suffered much.
With the man's suffering and she
understood.
Her heart filled with sorrow.
And her love unbending.

The woman still dreams to visit
the man.
Yet, she now carries the beauty
inside the fortress with her.
It was branded upon her heart.
A gift for her to keep.

Today, the woman looks to the
beauty inside her heart, which came
from the beauty inside the fortress,
and it is her art.
The art of bringing forth what is
inside — outside.

"I was 32 when I started cooking; up until then, I just ate."

—Julia Child

Everyone must sometime walk through the valley of sorrow. When sadness comes our way, what we all hurry to do is in someway shun the pain. Stay with it, feel it. Learn from it.

Cooking is a good remedial strategy. Allow yourself to be sad. Let your tears come and stream right into the dough, the sauce or the soup. Think about those things bringing you these feelings. Select which recipe you sense will bring you consolation. (personally, I always pick creamy, sweet things) Slowly your focus will shift off you and onto your cooking.

Gather the pots and pans you will need. Round up the ingredients and get started. Be mindful of the colors, textures and scents as you chop, cook and assemble. Foods are beautiful and luscious. God's purpose in making our nourishment tantalizing is so it will win our pleasure and satisfaction. Consider a summer peach! Beautifully round, warm soft skin, colored like a sunset and most inviting to take a bite.

Pour your heart into creating the dish you have chosen to prepare.
Be passionate! Soon enough delicious aromas will fill your kitchen and your spirit will rise.

However, the ultimate reward shall come from those with whom you share your heartfelt preparation and sadness will give way to joy. Thus by giving of yourself even in sorrow, Love shall return abundantly.

LOVE ENDURES ALL THINGS.... 1 COR 13:

Anne

93

Entrees

"Cooking is like love.
It should be entered into with abandon or not at all."
—Harriett Van Horne

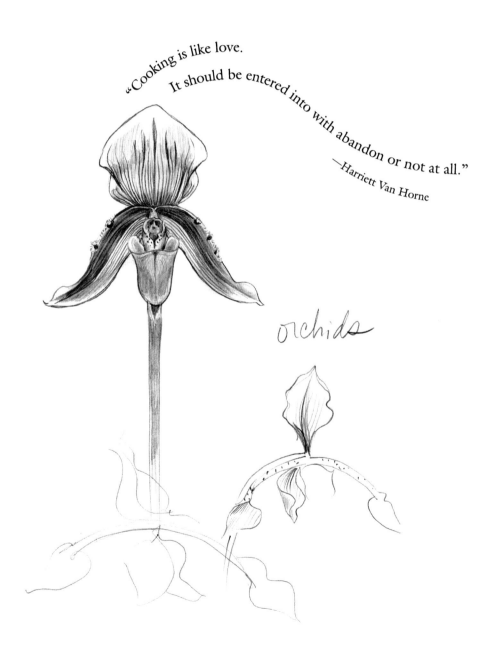

orchids

Blackened Salmon Fillet

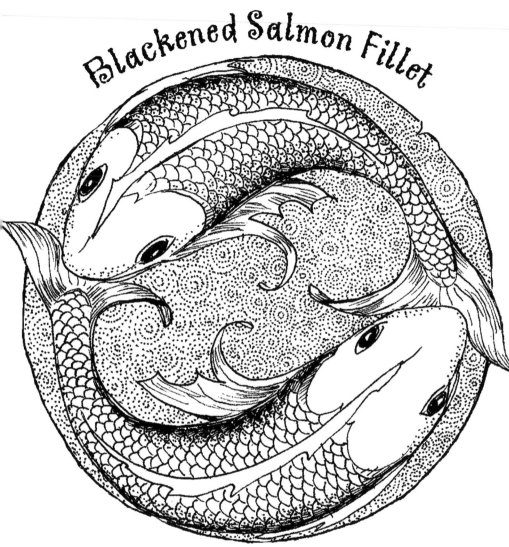

Preheat oven to 375°

Prepare a baking sheet with vegetable spray.

Place the salmon on the prepared sheet and cover generously with the blackening spice. Bake until salmon is opaque in middle, 15 to 25 minutes, depending on the thickness of the fillet.

Good to eat hot or cold over a salad.

6- to 8-oz. salmon fillet per person
Blackening spice (see recipe page 177)
Vegetable spray

Butternut Squash and Caramelized Onion Torte

3 lbs. butternut squash, cut in half, seeded, scraped free of membranes
Vegetable oil for greasing

2 tbl. olive oil
1 medium onion, chopped
8 large eggs
1 pint Silk soymilk creamer
1 tsp. sea salt
1 tsp. black pepper
½ tsp. nutmeg

Crust
1½ cups toasted almonds
1 cup white spelt flour
6 oz. almond butter
½ cup Silk soymilk creamer
½ tsp. sea salt

½ cup sliced almonds for topping

Preheat oven to 350°

Prepare a 9-inch springform pan with vegetable oil or spray.

Grease a baking pan (cookie sheet) with vegetable oil.

Place butternut squash cut side down on the greased baking sheet and roast until soft to the touch, approximately 35 to 40 minutes. Set aside.

Meanwhile prepare crust: Using food processor equipped with steel blade grind the almonds to a coarse crumb. Blend in the flour and almond butter. Scrape the sides of the bowl to loosen contents and add the soy creamer while pulsing. Blend to form dough. Use your fingers to press the almond dough up the sides of the pan first, then cover the bottom. Set aside.

Spoon out the flesh of the butternut halves and puree them in the food processor and puree. Set aside.

In a frying pan heat the olive oil and sauté the onion over low heat until caramelized. This may take 20 minutes.

Place the eggs in a mixing bowl and beat them to blend. Add the soy creamer, salt, pepper, nutmeg and blend well. Blend in the pureed butternut squash.

Place the caramelized onions in the bottom of the shell and pour the batter over them. Top with sliced almonds.

Place the pan on cookie sheet and bake until set, about 1 hour or until an inserted toothpick comes out clean. Remove from oven and let stand for 15 minutes before cutting.

Delicious with crisp green salad.

Chicken Enchiladas

Preheat oven to 350°

Prepare baking
pan with
vegetable spray.
Place chicken on
pan and dust with salt
and chili powder. (A little on
the heavy side for stronger flavor).
Bake for 20-25 minutes, or until done.
Cool, dice and set aside.

Quickly fry the tortillas in ¼-inch hot oil, turning to soften both sides. Remove promptly, drain on paper towels, and set aside.

In large mixing bowl blend sour cream, green onions and cilantro. (Reserve 1 tbl. chopped cilantro and 1 tbl. green onion). Mix in 1½ cups shredded jack cheese, chili powder, cumin and salt. Stir in diced chicken.

To assemble: place approximately 3-4 tablespoons of chicken mixture down the center of each fried tortilla. Roll up. Prepare an ovenproof baking dish with vegetable spray and spread a layer of green enchilada sauce over the bottom. Arrange the rolled up enchiladas, seam side down, in the baking dish; pour the remaining sauce over. Top with remaining shredded cheese and bake until cheese has melted, approx. 20-30 minutes. Garnish with reserved cilantro and green onion before serving.

1½ lbs.
  boneless, skinless
  chicken breasts
Salt to taste
Chili powder to taste
Vegetable spray

12 corn tortillas
Vegetable oil for frying

2 cups sour cream
4 green onions, chopped
½ cup chopped fresh cilantro
2 cups grated or shredded
  Monterey jack cheese
1 tbl. chili powder
1 tsp. cumin
½ tsp. salt

2 15-oz. cans Hatch green chile
  enchilada sauce (available at
  natural food stores), or other
  green enchilada sauce

Szechuan Tofu and Eggplant

1 cake (8-10 oz.) extra firm tofu, pressed dry and sliced vertically into ¼-inch pieces

Marinade for Tofu
2 tsp. toasted sesame oil
2 tbl. maple syrup
¼ cup tamari

4 Japanese eggplant, sliced into 1-inch rounds
3 tbl. olive oil

1 small red bell pepper roasted in the oven or canned, chopped coarsely

⅔ cup chopped cilantro
½ cup green onions, sliced

Sauce
½ cup tamari
1 tbl. minced ginger
3 cloves garlic, minced or pressed
⅓ cup maple syrup
½ cup water
1½ tbl. cornstarch
1 tsp. crushed red chilies
1 tbl. brown rice vinegar

Vegetable cooking spray

Preheat oven to 350°

Prepare the tofu. Whisk together the marinade ingredients. Spray a baking pan. Brush both sides of the tofu strips with marinade and arrange side by side in the baking pan. Pour remaining marinade over the tofu and bake for 15 minutes. Remove from oven and set aside.

While tofu is baking prepare the eggplant. Toss the eggplant rounds with the olive oil and arrange cut side up on a sprayed baking sheet. Bake until tender and very brown, about 35 to 40 minutes.

Place baked tofu and eggplant in a bowl and add the roasted red pepper.

Mix all the sauce ingredients except the vinegar. Whisk well to dissolve the cornstarch. Heat slowly, whisking constantly, until the cornstarch is cooked and the sauce has thickened. Sauce will become glossy and lose its cloudiness when cornstarch has been cooked long enough. Add the vinegar and taste. For a more sweet sauce add more maple syrup. For a more tart sauce add more vinegar. Pour sauce over the tofu/eggplant mixture. Add the cilantro, chopped green onion, and toss delicately.

Place in large saucepan to heat. Just before serving add cilantro and green onions.

Serve over steamed rice.

Mushroom and Goat Cheese Strudel

Preheat oven to 375°

Filling: best made a day ahead.

In a large skillet, heat the olive oil and add the chopped onion. Sauté until the onions are transparent. Add the mushrooms and sauté until they are tender and their liquid has evaporated, about 20 minutes. Add the garlic, salt and pepper.

Transfer to a mixing bowl and allow to cool.

When filling is cold, add the cheeses and the parsley. Mix gently.

Place filling in the center of the pastry lengthwise, ending 2 inches from the edges. Fold short sides in first, fitting tightly over the filling. Then fold the long sides in to form a packet. Press tight gently again to secure the filling.

Prepare a baking sheet with vegetable spray and place the strudel, seam side down, on the baking sheet. Brush with beaten egg. Use a sharp knife to make slight cuts in top to form a design and allow steam to escape. Bake for 20 minutes or until the pastry is golden brown and has puffed up.

½ cup chopped onion
2 tbl. olive oil
1½ lbs. very fresh white
  mushrooms, sliced
4 garlic cloves, pressed or minced
1 tsp. salt
1 tsp. black pepper
1 cup shredded mozzarella cheese
4 oz. crumbled goat cheese or feta
¼ cup chopped parsley

1 sheet frozen puff pastry, thawed
  but kept refrigerated until ready
  for use (available in frozen food
  aisle in most grocery stores)
1 beaten egg

Makes 2 to 3 servings

Quiche in Puff Pastry

1 sheet frozen puff pastry, thawed and kept cold until ready to use
Flour for rolling out dough

Filling
1 small onion, chopped
1 tbl. butter
4 eggs
1½ cups half-and-half
½ tsp. nutmeg
½ tsp. ground black pepper
1½ cups grated mozzarella or Swiss cheese
1 cup finely chopped broccoli blanched plus 1 cup sautéed mushrooms
OR
1½ cups finely chopped cooked spinach (omit the onion)

Other filling suggestions: sundried tomatoes, fresh tomatoes, olives, artichokes, leeks, caramelized onion, roasted peppers, roasted eggplant etc..

Preheat oven to 325°

Prepare a 9-inch pie pan with vegetable spray.

On a lightly floured surface, roll out puff pastry 1 inch larger than pan. Line the pie pan with the puff pastry. Press gently to cover the bottom and sides well and eliminate any air bubbles between the pan and the pastry. You may make folds if necessary. Use scissors to trim the pastry along the outer edge of the pan and remove the excess. Refrigerate until needed.

Sauté the onion in the butter until transparent. Set aside.

Beat the eggs until well blended; add the half-and-half and the seasonings. Mix well.

Place the onion in the prepared pan. Sprinkle with 1 cup of cheese. Top with the filling of your choice and cover with the remaining cheese. Place the pan on a cookie sheet and pour in the egg batter. Bake for 40-50 minutes, or until quiche no longer jiggles when shaken and toothpick inserted comes out clean.

Makes 8 servings

CAME TO DINNER . . .

102

Empanadas with Potato, Beans and Tofu

Preheat oven to 375°

Make pie crust as directed in recipe.

In a large sauté pan, heat the oil and cook chopped onion until transparent. Add diced potatoes and water, bring to a boil, lower heat and simmer, covered, until potatoes are tender, 10-15 minutes. Add drained beans, taco seasoning and salsa. Simmer for a few minutes longer until some of the liquid has evaporated.

While mixture is simmering, mash the tofu coarsely. Add the tofu to the potato mixture and heat thoroughly.

On a floured surface roll out the dough into 4 circles. Divide the filling among the 4 dough circles. Fold in half. Seal the packets by pressing a fork along the rounded edges.

Place each empanada on a baking sheet sprayed with vegetable spray.

Bake for 30 to 40 minutes or until the crust is golden brown.

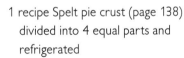

1 recipe Spelt pie crust (page 138) divided into 4 equal parts and refrigerated
1 medium yellow onion, chopped
2 tbl. olive oil
1 large baking potato, peeled and diced small
1 cup water
1 15-oz.can kidney beans, drained
1 package taco seasoning
1 16-oz.jar of your favorite salsa
8 oz. silken-style extra firm tofu
Vegetable spray

Chicken Pot Pies

One recipe of Spelt pie crust (page 138) or your favorite pie crust
4 5-inch foil pie pans
Vegetable spray

4 cups chicken broth
1 bay leaf
2 large boneless chicken breasts, skin on

½ cup chopped yellow onion
2 leeks, sliced thinly (white and pale green parts)
1 large carrot, diced
3 ribs celery, diced
1 large potato, peeled and diced

½ cup unbleached flour
½ cup water
1 tsp. ground black pepper
Salt to taste
½ cup heavy cream
¼ cup chopped parsley

1 egg, beaten, for eggwash

Preheat oven to 350°

Prepare pie crust—divide into 8 equal pieces and refrigerate until ready to use.

In a large, heavy-bottomed saucepan heat the chicken broth with the bay leaf. When starting to boil add the chicken, cover, and cook until done, about 25 minutes. Remove chicken and bay leaf from the broth. Set aside to cool.

Return broth to a boil and add the onion, leek, carrots, celery and simmer until almost tender, about 10 minutes. Add the potatoes and continue to simmer until the potatoes are fork tender, about 10 minutes. Remove from heat.

Mix flour and water to form a smooth paste, making sure mixture is free of clumps. Pour slowly into the soup while stirring well, being careful not to mash the potatoes but stirring firmly enough to incorporate the flour mixture without making lumps.

Season with the salt and pepper, and return to low heat. Simmer gently, stirring constantly to avoid sticking, until thickened, about 5 minutes.

Remove from heat and stir in the cream. Add the chopped parsley.

Skin and dice the chicken breasts. Add to the soup mixture and stir in.

Spray the foil pans.

On a floured surface, roll out the 8 pie crusts to fit the pans. Fill the pans with a bottom layer of crust. Fill each pan to the top with chicken filling and cover with top crust. Fold top crust under so it's a snug fit between the pan and the bottom crust.

Pinch the edges of the crust to form a scalloped edge.

Brush with egg wash and bake for 45 minutes or until they turn golden brown.

Hint: keep piecrust as cool as you can for easier manipulation.

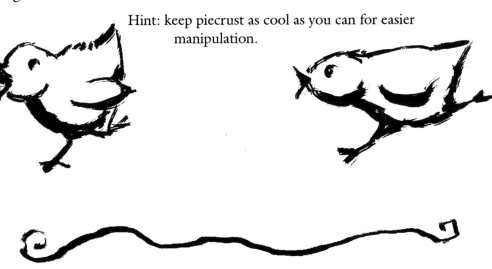

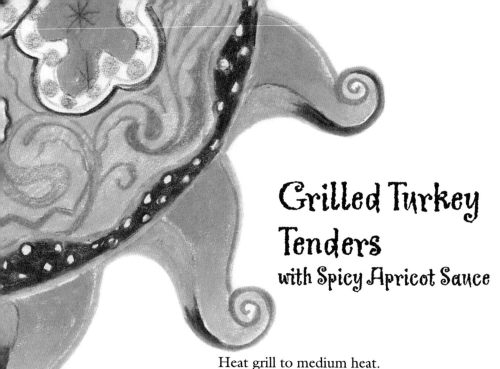

Grilled Turkey Tenders

with Spicy Apricot Sauce

½ lb. sulfured dried apricots
2 tsp. dried crushed red chilies
1 tsp. lemon juice
Sugar to taste, if needed
   (about 2 tsp.)
2 tsp. cornstarch
2 tsp. cold water

3 large turkey tenders
Olive oil
1 tbl. chili powder
½ tsp. salt

Heat grill to medium heat.

Place the apricots in a small saucepan and just cover with water. Add the red chilies and lemon juice. Bring to a boil, cover, lower heat and simmer until the apricots are very soft. Transfer to a food processor or blender and puree. Taste and add sugar if desired. Return to saucepan. Mix cornstarch with cold water to dissolve and quickly stir into the apricot sauce. Heat slowly, stirring constantly, until cornstarch loses its cloudiness and thickens. Transfer to mixing bowl and set aside.

Cut turkey tenders in half lengthwise along the center membrane. Remove membrane. Brush prepared tenders with olive oil; sprinkle with chili powder and salt. Place on the grill and cook 15 to 20 minutes, until no longer pink, turning them two or three times for even grilling. When done toss them in the apricot sauce.

6 servings

very good sliced. them over an organic mixed baby green salad!

106

Stuffed Baked Potatoes with Broccoli and Mushrooms

Preheat oven to 375°

Prepare a baking pan with vegetable spray.

Rub clean potatoes with olive oil so they are completely coated. Place on the baking pan and bake until they are fork tender, about 45 minutes to 1 hour. When done, set them aside to cool enough so you can handle them. Reduce oven heat to 350°.

While potatoes are baking, prepare the filling. Melt the butter in a large frying pan over low heat and add the chopped onion. Sauté until onion is transparent; add the broccoli florets and the sliced mushrooms. Cover and cook over low heat until the vegetables are tender. Transfer them to a large mixing bowl. Set aside.

Cut a thin slice, lengthwise, off the top of each potato and scoop the insides out into a separate bowl. The tops of the potatoes can be used as lids when they are served.

Mash the potato with the sour cream and shredded cheese and parsley. Season with salt and pepper. Adjust if more seasoning is needed. Fold in the broccoli/mushroom mixture and parsley. Fill the potato shells generously to form a mound above the rim. Top with more shredded cheese and bake at 350° until cheese topping is melted, 15-20 minutes.

4 extra large russet baking potatoes, scrubbed clean
Olive oil

Vegetable spray
3 tbl. butter
1 medium onion, chopped fine
1 lb. broccoli, cut into very small florets, stems discarded or saved for other recipes
8 oz. white button mushrooms, stems removed and sliced

1 cup sour cream
2 cups shredded cheddar cheese, plus extra for topping
½ cup chopped parsley
1 tsp. salt
1 tsp. ground black pepper

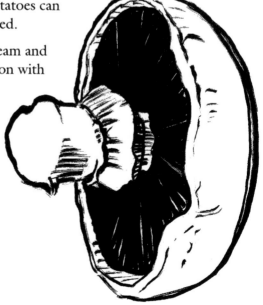

"SPRING-KEEPER'S COTTAGE AS A PART OF THE LARGE BOULDER, WHICH BECOMES THE BA[CK] WALL

Mustard Crusted Roast Beef

A top round, very lean, beef roast the size you need, about 8 ounces per serving

Blackening spice (see recipe page 177)

6-12 ounces quality Dijon mustard

Vegetable spray

Preheat oven to 500° for 15 minutes.

Rub the blackening spice generously all over the roast. Cover the roast with a good coat of mustard (well worth the mess).

Spray a baking pan with vegetable spray.

Place the roast on the pan and place in the very hot oven. Reduce the heat to 350°. For a rare roast cook 20 minutes per pound, for medium-rare cook 25 minutes per pound.

A very flavorful roast beef. Serve hot or cold, as a main course or sliced in sandwiches.

Turkey Meatloaf

2½ lbs. ground turkey
1 small onion, very finely chopped
1 red bell pepper, finely diced
1 carrot, peeled and grated
2 tsp. granulated garlic
1 tsp. ground black pepper
1½ tsp. salt
½ cup finely chopped parsley
1 cup organic ketch-up
⅓ cup organic Worcestershire
    sauce
3 eggs, lightly beaten
2 cups bread crumbs
¼ cup dried cranberries

Vegetable spray

Preheat oven to 325°

Prepare a 9x5-inch loaf pan with vegetable spray.

In a large mixing bowl blend all ingredients well. Use your hands for better mixing. Press into prepared loaf pan and smooth out top. Bake for one hour or until inside temperature reaches 145°. Allow to cool in the pan about 10 to 15 minutes before removal.

Roasted Butternut Squash
with Garlic and Rosemary

3 lbs. butternut squash peeled, seeded and cut into ½-inch cubes (select large ones to make peeling easier)
8-10 garlic cloves, peeled and left whole

¼ cup olive oil
1 tsp. salt
2 tsp. fresh rosemary or
   1 tsp. dried
Vegetable spray

Preheat oven to 350°

Peel the squash with very sharp knife or sharp vegetable peeler. Cut in half and scrape out the seeds. Cut off the bulbous end that holds the seeds and save for soup, pie or any recipe which calls for squash or sweet potato. Dice the solid part into ½-inch cubes and transfer to a mixing bowl. Add the peeled garlic cloves.

In a blender mix the oil, salt and rosemary. Blend until smooth, pour over the squash and garlic and toss.

Spray a baking sheet or pan with vegetable cooking spray and spread the squash and garlic evenly on the pan. Bake until soft and browned, 15-20 minutes.

Vegan Sweet Potato and Tofu Enchiladas

Preheat oven to 350°

In a large saucepan, heat the oil and sauté the chopped onion until transparent. Add garlic, chili powder and cumin, then add yams, chipotle pepper and the water. Stir to coat the yams. Cover and simmer until yams are soft and all water is absorbed, stirring frequently to avoid sticking. Add the tofu, green onions and cilantro and set aside.

Quick fry the tortillas in hot oil, turning to soften both sides. Drain on paper towels to remove excess oil.

Prepare a baking dish with vegetable oil. Coat with a layer of enchilada sauce. Spoon filling along center of each tortilla and roll up. Place the filled tortillas, seam side down, neatly in the dish. Cover with remaining sauce and bake for 20 minutes.

Garnish with cilantro, green onion, shredded cabbage or iceberg lettuce, diced tomatoes, diced red onion, diced jicama etc....

Note: This recipe is quite spicy.... For a less spicy dish you may cut back or omit altogether the chipotle pepper, but the flavor will change. Filling may also be made 24 hrs. ahead.

2 tbl. vegetable oil
1 medium onion, finely chopped
2 garlic cloves, minced or pressed
2 tsp. chili powder
1 tsp. ground cumin
2½ lbs. red-skinned yams, peeled and cubed into ½-inch pieces
1 chipotle pepper, chopped, plus 1 tsp. sauce (available in most markets, in Mexican foods section. Look for "Chipotle en Adobo")
¾ cup water
1 lb. firm tofu, well drained and mashed
4 green onions, sliced
1 bunch cilantro
Salt to taste

12 corn tortillas
Vegetable oil for frying
2 15-oz.cans Hatch green chili enchilada sauce or vegetarian enchilada sauce. (Your average brand enchilada sauce has a base of chicken stock. Vegan sauces are available at natural food stores)

Spring Rolls

In a large bowl, mix all the vegetables and the sesame seeds.

Using a blender, mix the dressing ingredients and pour over the vegetables. Toss, coating the vegetables well. Let sit for 5 minutes. Drain and reserve liquid.

Dust a flat surface with cornstarch. Place an egg roll sheet on the dusted surface with corner of sheet facing you (like a diamond). Top with enough vegetable mix for a well-filled spring roll, about ¼ cup, leaving enough space for secure rolling. Arrange vegetables in a strip horizontally across egg roll sheet from left corner to right corner stopping 1½-inch inch away from each corner.

Bring the southern point up over the filling to just below the northern point, then tuck this point tightly under the vegetables. Bring the left and right point toward the center to secure filling. Roll the egg roll toward the northern point and form an even spring roll. Secure point with cornstarch glue.

Place oil about 2 inches deep in frying pan. Heat until very hot. Test by dropping a small piece of vegetable into the oil. If the vegetable sinks, the oil is not hot enough. If the vegetable immediately sizzles and rises, remove promptly. Lower heat to medium and drop spring rolls one at a time into the hot oil. Depending on the size of your pan, fry 3 or 4 spring rolls at a time. Fry to brown one side then turn and brown other side. Continue this process until all spring rolls are fried. Drain on plate covered with paper towel to absorb excess oil.

3 cups finely shredded
 Napa cabbage
2 cups finely shredded
 green cabbage
⅔ cup shredded carrots
1 cup bean sprouts
1 tbl. toasted sesame seeds

Dressing
2 garlic cloves, minced or pressed
1 oz. fresh ginger, peeled and
 minced very fine
¼ cup tamari soy sauce
2 T. brown rice vinegar
2 T. Turbinado sugar

Egg roll sheets
1 tbl. cornstarch mixed with
 1 tbl. cold water for glue
A little cornstarch for dusting

Spectrum Naturals brand
Hi-oleic vegetable oil for frying.
(Other oils will work, but hi-oleic
oils burn less easily)

Risotto-Almond Loaf

1 small onion finely chopped

2 tbl. olive oil

3 garlic cloves, minced or pressed

1 tsp. dried basil

2 cups Arborio rice

4 cups vegetable broth

⅔ cup grated carrots

1 cup sliced almonds

2½ cups shredded mozzarella cheese

1 cup shredded Parmesan cheese

1 tsp. black pepper

1 tsp. salt

2 large eggs, beaten

Vegetable spray

Preheat oven to 325°

In a 3 qt. saucepan heat the oil and add the chopped onions. Sauté until onion is transparent. Stir in the garlic and basil. Add the Arborio rice and stir until the rice is well coated with oil. Add the broth and bring to boil. Cover and lower heat. Simmer until the rice has absorbed all the broth, 20-25 minutes. Transfer the rice into a mixing bowl, fluff and allow to cool. Add the remaining ingredients and fold in gently.

Grease a 9x5-inch loaf pan with vegetable spray and press the rice mixture evenly into the pan. Brush top lightly with olive oil. Bake at 325° for 1 hour. Allow to cool for 15 minutes and turn out of pan onto a serving plate.

Serve with a green salad for lunch or dinner.

Also great topped with sautéed mushrooms, vegetables or balsamic vinaigrette.

California Fuscia

Salmon Cakes

1½ lbs. salmon fillets
Blackening spice (see recipe
   page 177)
1 ear fresh corn
2 green onions, chopped
1 tsp. blackening spice
½ to ¾ cup Vegenaise
1 to 1½ cups bread
   crumbs

Preheat oven to 350°

Prepare 2 baking sheets with vegetable spray.

Place the salmon on the baking sheet skin side down. Cover generously with blackening spice. Bake until salmon is opaque in middle, 15 to 25 minutes, depending on the thickness of the fillet. Allow to cool.

When cooled, scrape away the gray fatty layer of the fillet. Place salmon meat in a mixing bowl and mash.

Remove the husk from the ear of corn and use a sharp knife to scrape the kernels off the cob into the bowl with the salmon. Add the chopped green onion, blackening spice and ½ cup Vegenaise. Mix well. If mixture is dry add more Vegenaise, a little at a time, until mixture is moist and holds together in a ball shape. Adding too much will make the mix too wet.

Place bread crumbs in a bowl. Use a 3 oz. ice cream scoop, if possible, or a large spoon to measure out enough mixture to make a ball 2 inches in diameter. Drop ball into bread crumbs and coat well. Take the coated ball in your hands and form a patty ½-inch thick. This is a rather messy procedure—do one at a time. Place patty on prepared baking sheet and bake for 20 minutes.

Serving suggestion: Place on top of a mixed green baby lettuce salad with your favorite dressing.

Makes 6 to 8 cakes.

Quick Pizza Crust

2 cups unbleached white flour
½ tsp. salt
½ tsp. sugar
1 tbl. active dry yeast
¾ cup hot water
2 tbl. olive oil

Place flour, salt, sugar and yeast in the bowl of a food processor fitted with steel blade and blend well. Add oil to hot water. Working quickly to avoid cooling of water, turn on the processor and pour the water through the feeding tube into the flour mixture. Blend until dough forms a ball. Stop machine and transfer dough onto a floured surface. Divide into 4 portions and roll out to desired thickness. Top with your favorite goodies and bake at 400° until crust is lightly browned and toppings are bubbly.

Makes 4 individual pizzas

Thai Coconut Rice

½ cup chopped onion
1 tbl. vegetable oil
3 garlic cloves, pressed
2 oz. fresh ginger, peeled and
  minced
½ tsp. salt
1 cups Arborio or Sushi rice

2 cups vegetable broth (use a tomato free broth. "Frontier Herb" meatless chicken broth powder is best—available at most natural foods stores)
1 14-oz. can Thai coconut milk
Grated zest (green part of rind) of 1 lime
1 tsp. crushed red chilies

In a 4-quart saucepan sauté the chopped onion in oil until it is transparent. Add garlic and ginger and salt and sauté 2 minutes longer over low heat. Add vegetable broth and rice; bring to a boil, cover and simmer until rice has absorbed broth, about 15-20 minutes.

When rice is ready add coconut milk, lime zest and crushed red chilies. Simmer, stirring frequently to prevent sticking, until thickened, about 5-7 minutes.

Delicious with shrimp, chicken or grilled vegetables.

Spinach and Toasted Pine Nut Tart

Crust

1½ cups toasted almonds
1 cup white spelt flour
6 oz. almond butter
½ cup Silk soymilk creamer
½ tsp. salt

8 large eggs
1 pint Silk soymilk creamer
1 tsp. salt
1 tsp. ground black pepper
½ tsp. nutmeg
3 10-oz. packages frozen organic chopped spinach, thawed and squeezed to remove excess water
½ cup pinenuts
Vegetable spray

Spray a 9-inch springform pan with vegetable spray, line the bottom with a circle of parchment paper, and spray paper.

Preheat oven to 350°

Prepare crust by grinding the almonds in a food processor fitted with a steel blade. Add the spelt flour and blend. Add the almond butter and blend. Add the soy creamer, salt, and blend until dough forms a ball. Use your fingers to press crust onto the sides of the springform pan, then over the bottom.

Beat eggs together. Add the soy creamer and seasonings; beat well. Add the spinach and blend well. Pour into the prepared crust and sprinkle the pinenuts on top.

Bake at 350° for about 1 hour or until set. Let tart sit for 15 minutes before serving.

Great with mixed green organic salad and marinated tomato slices.

The Ritz Garden, Ritz-Carlton, New York

Bombay Potatoes

In a large saucepan, heat the ghee and add the onion and ginger. Sauté until the onion is transparent. Add the diced potatoes, curry paste, salt, garlic and 1 cup of water. Simmer the potatoes until they are soft, 10-15 minutes. Check the water—if the water has evaporated before the potatoes are cooked add a little more. Stir in the garbanzo beans and tomatoes and heat well.

Serve with a sprinkle of chopped cilantro.

3 tbl. ghee or clarified butter (or vegetable oil for the vegans)

1 small onion, chopped

2 oz. fresh ginger, peeled and sliced into very thin, long strips

2 very large russet potatoes, peeled and diced into ½-inch cubes

3 tbl. Patak's mild curry paste (available in natural food stores and ethnic stores)

1 tsp. salt

4 garlic cloves, minced or pressed

1-1½ cups water

1 15-oz.can garbanzo beans, drained

1 14-oz. can diced organic tomatoes

¼ cup chopped cilantro

Vegan Millet and Rice Croquettes
with Shitake Mushrooms

1 tbl. olive oil
1 medium onion, chopped fine
(then divided in half)
½ cup millet
½ cup Arborio or sushi rice (or
any sticky style rice)
¼ cup dried cranberries (optional)
2½ cups vegetable broth

2 tbl. olive oil
1 lb. shitake mushrooms, stems
removed then sliced
1 tsp. rubbed sage
5 garlic cloves, minced or pressed

2 tbl. chopped parsley
Salt and pepper to taste
½ cup Silk soymilk creamer

Garlic flavored bread crumbs

Heat 1 tbl. olive oil in a saucepan. Add half the onion and sauté until onions are transparent. Add millet, rice and cranberries. Stir to coat well. Add broth and bring to a boil. Reduce heat, cover and simmer until all broth has been absorbed, about 20 minutes. While grains are cooking, heat 2 tbl. olive oil until soft in a skillet over medium heat. Sauté the remaining onions, shitake mushrooms, sage and garlic until onions are soft, about 10 minutes.

Transfer the cooked millet and rice into a mixing bowl. Add the cooked mushroom mixture. Add the parsley and season with salt and pepper to taste.

Add the soy creamer and mix lightly.

Prepare a cookie sheet with vegetable spray.

Place the bread crumbs in a bowl.

Use an ice cream scoop or a large serving spoon to form a ball for each croquette about 2 inches in diameter and drop it into the bread crumbs. Turn to coat well. Shape croquettes into long rectangles or leave in a ball shape. Place onto the prepared cookie sheet and bake for 20-30 minutes or until browned.

Serve with your favorite sauce such as sweet and sour sauce, roasted red pepper sauce or a marinara.

120

Salmon, Swiss Chard and Roasted Red Pepper Strudel

Preheat oven to 375°

Sauté onion in olive oil in a skillet over medium heat until tender and starting to brown. Add minced garlic and sauté for a few minutes longer. Add chopped Swiss chard and salt and cook, stirring often, until softened and limp, about 10 minutes. Transfer to colander and drain. Set aside to cool.

Drain and pat dry roasted red peppers.

Beat egg.

Assembly: Lay a 2 foot piece of parchment paper flat on work surface. Top with cold puff pastry sheet. Arrange well-drained Swiss chard mixture and spread to form a long strip lengthwise down the center, stopping approximately 3 inches away from the edge. Place cleaned salmon over Swiss chard, sprinkle with blackening spice and top with roasted red pepper.

Fold narrow ends over filling, then fold over the longer sides to form a tight package.

Place strudel seam side down on a baking sheet lined with parchment and sprayed with vegetable spray.

Brush pastry with beaten egg. Use a sharp paring knife to lightly cut a design in the pastry to let steam escape while it is baking. Bake for 20-25 minutes, until pastry is puffed and lightly browned.

Makes 2 servings

2 tbl. olive oil
1 very small onion, finely chopped (½ cup)
3 garlic cloves, pressed or minced
½ bunch Swiss chard, washed, stems removed and coarsely chopped
½ tsp. salt

2 large canned roasted red peppers
8 oz. salmon fillet, gray fat layer removed (if necessary) and kept whole
2 tsp. blackening spice (see recipe page 177)

1 egg, beaten
1 sheet frozen puff pastry, thawed but kept cold until ready to use (available in frozen section in most grocery stores)

Vegetable spray
Parchment paper
Baking sheet

Roasted Eggplant Bhaji

2½ lbs. Japanese eggplant, stems removed and sliced in 1-inch rounds

¼ cup olive oil

¼ cup ghee or clarified butter (or vegetable oil for the vegans)

1 medium onion, chopped

½ cup Patak's mild curry paste (available at natural food stores or ethnic markets)

2 tsp. ground coriander

1 tsp. ground cumin

1 28-oz. can organic diced tomatoes, with juice

Salt to taste

Vegetable spray

Preheat oven to 375°

Spray a cookie sheet with vegetable spray.

In a large mixing bowl toss sliced eggplant with olive oil and salt until well coated. Place eggplant, cut side up, on prepared baking sheet. Place in oven and roast until well browned, about 45 minutes.

While eggplant is roasting, heat ghee in a large saucepan. Add onion, curry paste, coriander, cumin and cook until onion is soft. Add the tomatoes and simmer until flavors are well blended, about 15 minutes. Toss in the roasted eggplant and stir gently. Taste and add salt if necessary.

Barbecued Baked Soybeans

Casserole

Boil soybeans in one quart of the water for 5 minutes. Turn off the heat and let stand for 30 minutes. Skim off the foam, drain, and return beans to the pot with the remaining one quart water. Cook until the beans are soft, about 90 minutes. Drain and set aside.

Mix together onion, garlic, BBQ sauce, brown sugar, molasses, mustard and mix with the beans. Transfer to an ovenproof baking dish. Cover and bake at 300° for about 2 hours, stirring occasionally. Add water if beans get too dry, or uncover if beans remain soupy.

2 cups dried soybeans
2 quarts water, divided

1 medium onion chopped
3 cloves garlic
1 cup of your favorite BBQ sauce
½ cup brown sugar
⅓ cup molasses
2 tbl. Dijon mustard

"Food without hospitality is medicine." —Tamil proverb

Love Is Not Proud

Love is inclusive, on the other hand, pride is exclusive. Pride manifests itself as the wall that keeps selfless love from being revealed. Pride is the thing that will prevent us from embracing what life and love want to teach us. Pride has many nuances, names and disguises. Whatever name we give to it, we wrap ourselves in it very tightly, disabling our hearts from being open and vulnerable to receive the gifts God has to offer.

Pride blocks creativity as well. It leaves you feeling frozen and overly cautious, for fear of looking bad, acting wrong, or being unacceptable. This also happens in cooking. Bringing your personal touch to a recipe is what gives your cooking its personality. Savory cooking is very resilient, so go ahead and leave out an ingredient that's not available, or add something you feel will enhance the flavor or texture of the food. If it doesn't work out then try again next time with a little more wisdom. Let it be an encouraging reminder not to be afraid to make mistakes and see it as adding a pinch of yourself instead. A meal or a single dish created in humility is far more heartwarming than a plate served in vanity. The life-giving force of love is what gives our food its regenerative power.

Anne

Desserts

Helianthus

"The more you praise and celebrate your life,
the more there is in life to celebrate."
—Oprah Winfrey

Gammy's Fudge Brownies

Preheat oven to 375°

Melt butter and unsweetened chocolate in 2-quart saucepan over low heat until melted and smooth. Remove pan from heat and mix in sugar. Add eggs, one at a time, then vanilla and salt. Stir in flour and mix well.

Pour batter into greased 8-inch square pan; sprinkle chocolate chips evenly over the top. Bake for 25 minutes—no longer! These are chewy and moist, but horribly dry and awful if overbaked. Let brownies cool before cutting into 9 squares.

½ cup (1 stick) butter
2 oz. unsweetened baking chocolate
1 cup sugar
2 eggs
1 tsp. vanilla
Pinch salt
¾ cup flour
½ cup (3 oz.) chocolate chips

Party
English Trifle
Wheat-free

This dessert is best presented in a classic trifle dish (a footed glass bowl with straight sides) but any see-through glass dish will do.

Make breakfast cake (preferably made one or two days ahead).

Using a food processor equipped with a steel blade, blend the tofu and the instant pudding mix. Run machine for a few minutes until mixture is very smooth, scraping sides often. Set aside.

Wash all the fruit and set aside the blueberries. Halve the peaches, remove pits and peel if desired; slice thinly. Cut the strawberries in half; set aside.

Slice the breakfast cake in half lengthwise then crosswise into half-inch slices.

Arrange all your ingredients in front of you for easy assembling.

Begin by placing sliced peaches in a circle on the bottom of the dish. Reserve a few for decoration. Pour ½-cup pineapple juice over the peaches. Use half the cake to arrange slices in a circle over the peaches, starting at the outer edge first, overlapping like fallen dominos. Fill center in the same manner. Pour half the remaining pineapple juice over the cake. Spread half the tofu mixture evenly over the cake. Sprinkle with all the blueberries. Press strawberry halves all around with cut side out against the glass dish. They can set slightly into the pudding. Place the remaining cake over the blueberries within the strawberry circle. Pour remaining pineapple juice over the cake. Spread remaining tofu mixture over the cake. Arrange remaining peaches and strawberries over the top in decorative fashion, then sprinkle with the toasted almonds.

Serves 12 to 15

1 5 qt. glass bowl or trifle dish
1 Lemon Breakfast Cake (page 135) or North African
Almond and Saffron Breakfast Cake (page 146)
*It is preferable to make the breakfast cake a day ahead as
it will slice better*
3 packages Mori-Nu instant vanilla pudding
3 packages extra firm silken-style tofu
2 ripe peaches or nectarines
1½ cups fresh or frozen blueberries
4 cups strawberries
2 cups pineapple juice
1 cup toasted almonds, chopped

Scones

3 cups unbleached flour
1½ tsp. baking powder
½ cup turbinado sugar
1 stick butter (cold), cut into
  8 pieces
½ tsp. salt
1 to 1¼ cup heavy whipping
  cream
1 tsp. vanilla extract

1 cup of any of the following:
  chopped nuts,
  dried fruit, finely diced
  fresh or frozen fruit

Preheat oven to 350°

Place the dry ingredients in the bowl of a food processor equipped with a steel blade. With motor running, add butter pieces through the feed tube. Run until butter is completely incorporated into the flour and mix resembles coarse meal. This happens very quickly; do not over-process.

Transfer into a mixing bowl and add cream, vanilla and flavoring. Fold together using a rubber spatula or large spoon until dough holds together into one ball.

Transfer onto floured surface and form an even 8-inch circle. Cut into 12 wedges. Place in a pie pan or on cookie sheet sprayed with vegetable spray. Bake for 25 minutes or until dough springs back when indented with your finger.

Rachel's Apricot Oatmeal Cookies
with Barley Flour

Preheat oven to 350°

Prepare a cookie sheet with vegetable spray.

Using a mixer fitted with a paddle, cream butter and fructose together until light and fluffy. Add eggs and vanilla. Mix until smooth, scraping down sides of the bowl occasionally. Add flour, salt, soda, oats and mix until blended. Add chopped apricots and mix.

Divide dough into twelve balls. Place on prepared cookie sheet and flatten lightly with the heel of your hand.

Bake for 15-20 minutes or until golden.

Makes 1 dozen 3-inch cookies.

1 cup (2 sticks) butter
2 cups fructose
2 eggs
1 tsp. vanilla
2½ cups barley flour
½ tsp. salt
1 tsp. baking soda
2½ cups rolled oats
10 dried organic, unsulphured
    apricots, finely chopped

No Dairy - No Wheat Pumpkin Pie

Vegetable spray
Half recipe Spelt Pie Crust (page 138)
1 small can pumpkin (12 to 14 ounces)
1 cup turbinado sugar
½ tsp. salt
2 tsp. cinnamon
½ tsp. nutmeg
2 eggs
12 oz. Silk soymilk creamer (available at most natural food stores)
1 tbl. vanilla extract

Preheat oven to 425°

Prepare spelt pie crust, using soy margarine instead of butter.

Spray a 9-10-inch pie pan with vegetable spray. Roll out dough slightly larger than pie pan. Press dough evenly into pan. Use a knife to cut around the outer edge of pan to remove excess dough. Scallop the rim of dough with fingers or press a fork around edge to form a design. Excess dough can also be used for garnish using tiny cookie cutters for desired shapes.

In a mixing bowl beat the pumpkin, sugar, salt, cinnamon and nutmeg until well mixed. Add eggs one at a time, beating well after each addition. Mix in soy creamer and vanilla.

Place lined pie pan on a baking sheet. Pour the batter into the prepared pie shell and place in oven on middle rack. Reduce oven temperature to 325° and bake for 45-55 minutes or until the center no longer looks runny when shaken.

Lemon Breakfast Cake
Wheat free

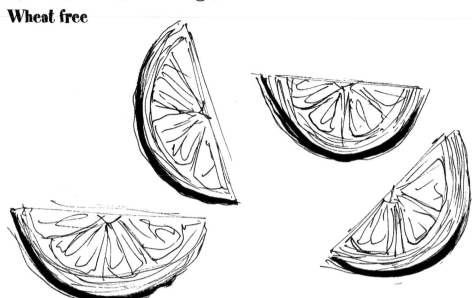

Preheat oven to 350°

Prepare a 2 lb. loaf pan (approx. 4x8 inches) with vegetable spray. Line pan with parchment paper and spray again.

Sift together the dry ingredients. A food processor may be used.

In a mixer bowl whisk the egg with whipping attachment until light in color and frothy. Stop mixer and add the dry ingredients, the zest and the wet ingredients. Beat mixture, scraping sides occasionally, for one minute. Pour into prepared pan and bake until an inserted toothpick comes out clean, about
35 to 45 minutes.

2 cups white spelt flour
 (see note)
1 cup turbinado sugar
1 tsp. baking powder
½ tsp. sea salt
Zest of 1 organic lemon,
 very finely chopped
1 egg
½ cup buttermilk
½ cup vegetable oil
2 tsp. pure lemon extract

– whole SPELT FLOUR may be used for a heartier cake –

135

Cinnamon Rolls
Vegan

1 cup very warm water
(98° to 110°)
¼ cup turbinado sugar
2 tbl. active dry yeast

1 cup very warm water
(98° to 110°)
1 cup vegetable oil
1 cup turbinado sugar
1 tsp. salt
1 tbl. vanilla

3 cups unbleached all-purpose
flour
Egg replacer equivalent to 3 eggs
(as per instructions on the box)
4 to 5 cups unbleached
all-purpose flour

1 cup cinnamon sugar (1 cup sugar
+ ¼ cup cinnamon)

Glaze
2 cups powdered sugar
4 to 6 tbl. Silk soymilk creamer

Stir the first three ingredients in the mixing bowl of an electric mixer equipped with a dough hook or a paddle. Mix lightly—just enough to moisten the yeast. Allow to stand for 3-5 minutes to dissolve the yeast completely.

Add the next five ingredients and blend. Add the three cups of flour and mix, then beat until the dough becomes elastic. Dough will still be very sticky.

Add the egg replacer and blend until well incorporated. With the machine on, add the additional flour ½ cup at a time until the dough forms a soft ball pulling away from the sides of the bowl. Transfer to a well-floured surface and knead, adding more flour as needed until the dough is no longer sticky but still soft. Form dough into a ball.

Transfer dough to a greased bowl, cover with plastic wrap and place in a warm area to rise. Allow to rise for 30 minutes or until doubled in size.

Turn risen dough once again onto a floured surface and punch down. Roll dough out to a large rectangle (about 2½ feet by 1½ feet). Brush surface completely with vegetable oil and sprinkle with the cinnamon sugar. Roll up starting at the longer side to form a log. Cut into twelve disks or eighteen disks depending upon thickness of slices.

Place in greased baking pan or a muffin pan fitted with greased cupcake liners. Brush tops with a little oil and return to the warm spot to allow to rise again until doubled in size, approximately 30 minutes.

Bake at 350° until browned and cooked on the inside, about 30 to 40 minutes. Remove from oven and cool.

Mix glaze ingredients together and beat until smooth and free of lumps. Pour over cinnamon rolls.

Makes 12 large rolls or 18 medium

Spelt Pie Crust
Vegan - Wheatfree

Makes two 9-inch pie shells or one top and one bottom

3 cups white spelt flour
½ tsp. baking powder
½ tsp. salt
2 sticks soy margarine or canola margarine (cut into small cubes)
⅓ to ½ cup ice water

Place the dry ingredients in the bowl of a food processor fitted with a steel blade. Blend briefly. Remove the lid and scatter the margarine cubes evenly over the flour mixture. Replace the lid and pulse in the margarine quickly until it resembles course meal, taking care not to over process Remove the lid again and pour the ice water evenly over this mixture. Replace the lid and pulse the processor just until a ball forms. If the dough forms uneven crumbles, add a little water.

Remove the ball from the processor onto a floured surface and roll it even. Cut in two and flatten each half into a disk. Wrap each disk in plastic wrap and refrigerate for at least one hour before rolling out. Dough will keep for two to three days.

Anne's Carrot Cake

Preheat oven to 350°

Generously grease and flour 2 9-inch cake pans or 2 8-inch cake pans for taller cake. Set aside.

In a large bowl mix the dry ingredients with a whisk.

Beat the eggs in a separate bowl. Add the oil, buttermilk, sugar, and vanilla and beat to blend. Add to flour mixture with pineapple, carrots, coconut and chopped nuts. Fold together until mixture is well moistened. Do not beat. Pour into prepared pans.

Bake 45 minutes or until the cake starts to pull away from the side of the pans and a tester inserted comes out clean.

Cool in the pan for 5 minutes, remove from the pans and cool completely before frosting.

While cake is baking make the frosting: Whip the butter and cream cheese until blended. Add the vanilla and the powdered sugar and beat again. Mix in the orange peel and juice.

1½ cups unbleached all purpose flour
1½ cups whole wheat pastry flour
1 tsp. baking soda
2 tsp. baking powder
4 tsp. cinnamon
½ tsp. salt
4 eggs
1 cup vegetable oil
1 cup buttermilk
2 cups turbinado sugar
2 tsp. vanilla extract
1 8-oz. can crushed pineapple, drained
2 cups grated carrots
1½ cups shredded coconut
1 cup pecans or walnuts, coarsely chopped

Cream Cheese Frosting

1 stick butter, at room temperature
2 8-oz. packages cream cheese, at room temperature
2 tsp. vanilla extract
3 cups powdered sugar
1 tbl. grated orange peel
1 tsp. orange juice

over local. walnut

green and brown & black skin reveals a perfect brown nut!

Apple Cranberry
upside down cake

1½ sticks (¾ cup) butter, at room temperature
½ cup packed brown sugar

8 very small Granny Smith apples, peeled, cored and halved
1 cup cranberries

1½ cups unbleached flour
1 tsp. cinnamon
1 tsp. baking powder
¼ tsp. baking soda
¾ cup turbinado sugar
1 tsp. vanilla
3 large eggs
½ cup sour cream

Vegetable spray

Preheat oven to 350°

Prepare an 8-9-inch springform pan with vegetable spray. Line with parchment paper, cutting a circle to fit the bottom, then a strip for the sides, making sure the edges of the bottom and sides overlap a little. Spray again.

Melt ½ stick (4 tbl.) butter and mix with the brown sugar. Spread over the bottom of the prepared pan. Arrange apples over the sugar mixture, cut side up, in a circle around the edge, then fill in the center with remaining apples. Fill the gaps with cranberries. Set aside.

In a large bowl mix all dry ingredients except sugar. In bowl of mixer with paddle attachment, beat sugar, vanilla and remaining butter until fluffy. Beat in eggs one at a time. Alternately mix in flour mixture with sour cream.

Pour batter over fruit and bake for 50-60 minutes or until an inserted knife comes out clean.

Allow to cool for 5 minutes. Run a knife along the sides to detach. Remove the side of the pan and invert onto a serving platter. Remove the disk and paper.

Serve warm.

140

Thumbprints

Preheat oven to 375°

Beat butter until smooth; mix in sugar or
fructose or honey. Beat in egg yolks, one at
a time. Add vanilla and zest, then flour and
salt. Mix well.

Place egg whites in small bowl. Beat with
fork until foamy.

Place chopped nuts in another small bowl.

Shape cookie dough into 1-inch balls. Dip
half of dough ball into egg whites, then
into nuts. Place on cookie sheets, nut side
up, 2 inches apart. Flatten slightly. Bake for
5 minutes. Use a ½ tsp. measuring spoon
to make a deep indentation in the tops of
cookies (cookies may crack, that's OK).
Fill each indentation with 1 teaspoon jam.
Return to oven and bake 8 minutes longer,
until edges are light brown. Cool on racks.

Makes about 2 dozen

1 cup butter (2 sticks), softened
½ cup brown sugar, fructose or
   honey
2 eggs, separated
1 tsp. vanilla
½ tsp. orange zest, finely grated
   (orange part only of orange
   peel)
2 cups flour
¼ tsp. salt
½ cup walnuts or pecans, finely
   chopped
½ cup jam of your choice,
   strawberry, apricot or raspberry
   are good choices

141

Oatmeal Cranberry Cookies

½ cup butter, softened
½ cup honey
1 large egg
1 tsp. finely grated orange zest
1 cup unbleached or whole wheat flour
1 tsp. baking soda
1½ cups rolled oats
½ cup dried cranberries
Note: dried cherries, blueberries, or raisins may be substituted

In a mixing bowl, beat butter and honey together until creamy. Beat in egg and orange zest. Stir in flour and baking soda. Mix in oats and cranberries and blend well. Drop dough by rounded teaspoonfuls onto greased or parchment lined cookie sheets, about 2-inch apart. Bake for 8-10 minutes, until lightly browned. Remove to racks to cool.

Makes about 3 dozen

Raspberry Hazelnut Bars

3 sticks (1½ cups) butter, room temperature
1⅔ cups sugar
2 eggs
3¾ cups all-purpose flour (or spelt or barley flour)
1½ cups (about 7 oz.) chopped, toasted hazelnuts
2 cups raspberry preserves

Note: apricot preserves or orange marmalade are delicious also

Heat the oven to 350°. Butter a 9x13-inch pan. In bowl of electric mixer, cream the butter and sugar until fluffy. Add the eggs one at a time, beating well after each addition. Add the flour and mix just enough to incorporate. Add the nuts and mix a little longer until just blended.

Press about two-thirds of the mixture into the prepared pan. Spread with the preserves and then crumble the remaining dough on top. Bake for about 1 hour, until the top is lightly browned. Cool and cut.

Yields about 48 bars

Giant Muffins

Preheat oven to 350°

Prepare a muffin pan with paper muffin pan liners and spray with vegetable spray.

In a large mixing bowl, whisk together the dry ingredients.

In a separate bowl whisk together the wet ingredients. Pour into the dry ingredients. Add fruit, nuts and/or flavorings and use a rubber spatula to fold together just until dry ingredients are well moistened, as overbeating will result in a chewy muffin. Use an ice-cream scoop to fill each muffin well to the top creating a mound.

Bake for 25-30 minutes, until a tester inserted comes out clean.

Makes 12 to 15 extra large muffins

4 cups white spelt flour
2 cups old fashioned oats
1½ cups turbinado sugar
2 tsp. baking powder
½ tsp. baking soda
1 tsp. salt

4 large eggs
1 cup vegetable oil
1 cup buttermilk
2 tsp. vanilla

Optional flavorings:
Add fresh or frozen fruit (about 2 cups worth) such as berries, peaches, or mango.
Add 1 cup pumpkin or mashed sweet potatoes, reduce oil and buttermilk by ¼ cup each. Add 1 tsp. cinnamon to dry ingredients
Replace oil with applesauce for lower fat muffins
Replace vanilla with almond extract and add 3 tbl. poppyseeds for almond poppyseed muffins
Add 2 tsp. flaxseed if you'd like.

Add 2 cups shredded carrot or zucchini and 1 tsp. cinnamon
For carrot cake muffins add 1 cup shredded carrot, ½ cup crushed pineapple and ½ cup coconut flakes. Add cinnamon to dry ingredients
Add 2 cups fresh or frozen cranberries and replace vanilla with orange extract

Anne's Famous Coconut Cake

4 eggs

2 cups sugar

2½ cups unbleached all-purpose flour

2 tsp. baking powder

1 tsp. salt

1 cup light vegetable oil

1 cup dry white wine or buttermilk

1 tbl. vanilla

Zest of ½ lemon

Vegetable spray

Preheat oven to 350°

Prepare two 9-inch cake pans with vegetable spray. Dust bottom and sides with flour, removing excess by gently tapping the flour out of the pans.

In mixer bowl, beat eggs and sugar on high speed until mixture is light and frothy. Turn off mixer and add flour, baking powder, salt, oil, wine or buttermilk, vanilla and lemon zest. Beat 2 minutes on high speed.

Pour batter into the cake pans, dividing it evenly, and bake 40 minutes or until an inserted toothpick comes out clean.

Cool cakes completely before filling and frosting.

I WOULD IF I COULD BUT I CAN'T.

This cake is not called Anne's FAMOUS for no reason!

144

Vanilla Pastry Cream Filling

Better made a day ahead, and more convenient too!

In a 2-quart saucepan heat the milk and vanilla to a boil and keep hot.

Using mixer, beat sugar and egg yolks together until fluffy and pale in color. Reduce speed and slowly incorporate the cornstarch, beat until well blended.

Pour the hot milk into the sugar mixture while beating continuously. When well blended return the mixture to the saucepan and heat slowly, stirring continually to prevent mixture from sticking to the bottom of the pan. Continue cooking until filling becomes very thick.

Pour mixture into a bowl, cover with plastic wrap and set aside to cool.

When completely cooled, combine vanilla pastry cream with mascarpone cheese to form thick filling.

Spread filling between two cake layers.

Frosting: Whip cream until thick (add sugar when cream is slightly thickened, if needed)

Spread whipped cream over sides and top of cake. Press coconut flakes into whipped cream to cover cake.

1⅓ cups milk
1 tbl. vanilla
6 egg yolks
1 cup granulated sugar
4 tbl. cornstarch
1 lb. mascarpone cheese or cream cheese* (drain off any liquid resting on top of mascarpone cheese if necessary)

*mascarpone cheese is far better, but if unattainable cream cheese will do

Frosting
2 cups heavy cream
3 cups sweetened coconut flakes*

*If using unsweetened coconut flakes, add ½ cup powdered sugar to the cream midway through whipping

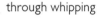

145

North African Almond and Saffron Breakfast Cake
Wheat-free

2 cups white spelt flour
1 cup turbinado sugar
1 tsp. baking powder
½ tsp. sea salt
10 strands saffron, crushed

1 egg
½ cup buttermilk
½ cup vegetable oil
1 tbl. pure almond extract

½ cup toasted almonds, chopped

Preheat oven to 350°

Prepare a 2 lb. loaf pan with vegetable spray, line with parchment paper and spray again.

Sift together the dry ingredients and stir in the saffron. A food processor may be used.

In the bowl of a mixer whisk the egg with the whipping attachment until the egg is frothy and light in color. Stop the mixer, add the wet and dry ingredients. Beat, scraping the sides occasionally, for one minute.

Pour into prepared pan. Sprinkle top of batter with almonds and press down lightly. Bake for 35 - 45 minutes or until an inserted toothpick comes out clean.

Missy's Cheesecake Brownies

Preheat oven to 350°

Brownies - Melt butter and chocolate in a medium saucepan. Remove from heat and add sugar. Beat in eggs. Add flour and vanilla and mix well. Set aside.

½ cup butter
2 oz. unsweetened chocolate
1 cup sugar
2 eggs
¾ cup flour
1 tsp. pure vanilla

Filling - Beat cream cheese until smooth and creamy. Beat in sugar, then egg. Add flour and cream, mix well.

8 oz. cream cheese
⅓ cup sugar
1 egg
1 tbl. flour
1 tbl. whipping cream

Line an 8-inch round cake pan with aluminum foil. Smooth foil carefully to eliminate creases. Spray foil with cooking spray. Spread all but ½-cup of brownie batter into prepared pan. Pour cheesecake batter over brownie. Drop spoonfuls of remaining brownie batter over cheesecake. With tip of knife, swirl filling gently. Bake for about 40 minutes, just until brownies are done when a toothpick inserted in middle comes out clean. *Do not overbake.* Remove from oven and cool. Refrigerate until cold and cut into 6-10 wedges.

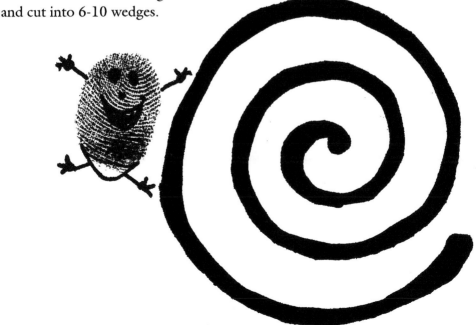

Vegan Rice Pudding

1 cup Arborio rice
2 cups water
½ tsp. salt
3 cups Silk soymilk creamer
¾ cup sugar
1 tbl. vanilla extract, or 1 vanilla
   bean split in half and seeds
   scraped out

Using a heavy-bottomed saucepan, boil the rice in the water until water has been absorbed, about 20 minutes. Inserting a knife in the center of the rice and pushing the rice aside a little will allow you to see how much water remains.

Add the creamer (if using vanilla bean add now) and stir to incorporate. Simmer slowly, stirring very frequently to avoid sticking to the bottom of the pan. When rice has thickened (about another 20 to 25 minutes), add the sugar and the vanilla. Stir and continue to simmer until sugar is dissolved.

Serve with fresh sliced fruit. Delicious when served while still warm.

Just like mom used to make

Chocolate-Peanut Butter Vegan Brownies

Preheat oven to 350°

In a medium mixing bowl, sift together the flour, cocoa, and baking powder and salt; set aside.

Place the tofu in the bowl of a food processor fitted with a knife blade. Process until tofu is creamy. Add oil, chocolate, applesauce, peanut butter, maple syrup, Sucanat or sugar, and vanilla. Process until mixture is smooth and creamy. Add tofu mixture to the flour mixture in bowl and mix well. Stir in chocolate chips. Spread in a 9x13-inch pan sprayed with nonstick vegetable spray. Bake for 25-30 minutes, until brownies are set in middle.

Makes 12

¾ cup unbleached flour
¼ cup cocoa powder
¼ tsp. baking powder
½ tsp. salt
4 oz. silken-style soft tofu (6 tbl.)
5 tbl. canola oil
2 oz. unsweetened chocolate, melted
½ cup applesauce
6 tbl. peanut butter
½ cup maple syrup
½ cup Sucanat (granulated cane juice), or turbinado sugar
2 tsp. vanilla extract
2 cups (12 oz.) chocolate chips, such as Tropical Source or Sunspire brand

Rachel's Wheat-free German Chocolate Cake

Cake

3 cups spelt flour
1¼ tsp. baking soda
¼ tsp. salt
1 cup granulated sugar
1 cup butter
1 tsp. vanilla
3 egg yolks
1 cup semi-sweet chocolate chips,
  melted
1¼ cups buttermilk
3 egg whites
½ cup granulated sugar

Preheat oven 350°

Grease and flour lightly three 8-inch cake pans.

In a small bowl mix the flour, baking soda and salt.

Using a mixer fitted with a paddle, mix 1 cup sugar and the butter. Beat until light and fluffy. Add egg yolks one at a time. Scrape down sides after adding the eggs and mix in the melted chocolate chips and vanilla until just blended. Add flour mixture and buttermilk alternately, beginning and ending with flour.

Using a very clean bowl beat the egg whites and ½ cup sugar until stiff peaks form. Fold the beaten egg whites into the chocolate mixture.

Divide the batter into the three prepared cake pans and bake for 25 to 35 minutes or until an toothpick inserted comes out dry. Let cool for five minutes in the pans, then invert pans onto cooling racks and drop out the cakes. Allow cakes to cool completely before frosting.

Johnny-Jump-Up (yellow)
Viola-Penduncula

↑ Larvae of the Silver spot butterfly (Speyeria) feed on these

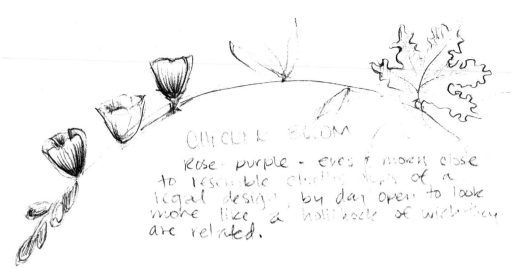

CHICORY BLOOM

Rose purple - eyes & morn close
to resemble chellin[?] of a
legal design, by day open to look
more like a hollihock or which they
are related.

Prepare Frosting: In a large saucepan melt the butter, heavy cream and Yellow "D" sugar. Remove from heat.

Beat the egg yolks and add ½ cup of very hot butter/cream mixture (stirring fast so the eggs do not curdle) then pour hot egg mixture back into the butter/cream mixture, stirring constantly to avoid curdling. Return to heat and cook, stirring constantly, over low flame until mixture thickens, 15 to 20 minutes.

Remove from heat and add vanilla, coconut and pecans; stir well and refrigerate to cool. When cooled, spread between layers of cake and over the top only, leaving sides bare.

Prepare ganache glaze: Melt the chocolate chips and the cream, stirring mixture vigorously to blend and form a smooth glaze.

Pour glaze over the outer edge of cake top, forming a ring on the top of the cake, letting glaze run down the sides. Use a frosting spatula or broad knife for smooth, even coating.

Allow cake to set in the fridge before slicing.

Frosting and Filling

1 cup butter

2 cups heavy cream

2 cups Yellow "D" sugar (available at natural food stores) or brown sugar

6 egg yolks

1 tsp. vanilla extract

2 cups coconut flakes

2 cups pecans

Ganache Glaze

4 cups chocolate chips

2 cups heavy cream

Swedish White Brownies

2 eggs
1 cup sugar, plus additional for
  sprinkling on top
½ cup butter, melted and cooled
1 cup flour
½ tsp. almond extract
½ cup chopped pecans

Preheat oven to 325°

In a medium mixing bowl, beat eggs well. Add sugar and beat again. Mix in melted butter, then flour and extract. Stir in pecans. Pour into greased 8-inch square pan, sprinkle top with granulated sugar. Bake for 30-35 minutes, until brownies are set.

Cut into squares when cool.

Makes 9-12

Good Old-Fashioned Chocolate Chip Cookies

2½ cups unbleached flour
1½ tsp. baking soda
1 tsp. salt
¾ cup white sugar
¾ cup brown sugar
2¼ cups chocolate chips
1 cup (2 sticks) butter
2 large eggs
1 tbl. vanilla

Preheat oven to 375°

Place first six ingredients in a large mixing bowl. Set aside.

Melt butter in microwave in a large (4-cup) glass measuring cup or in a small saucepan on the stovetop. Set aside to cool slightly, 5-10 minutes.

Add eggs and vanilla to melted butter and mix well. Pour over dry ingredients and stir to blend;- you may need to use your hands.

Place dough on cookie sheets by large tablespoonfuls. Flatten to ¼-inch high. Bake for 9-12 minutes, until golden brown.

Makes 4 dozen cookies.

Famous Lemon Bars

Preheat oven to 350°

For crust: beat butter and powdered sugar until creamy and smooth. Add salt and flour and mix well. Press into greased 9x13-inch baking pan. Bake 20 minutes.

While crust is baking mix all filling ingredients until smooth, pour over top of hot crust. Bake for 20-25 minutes, until filling is set. Remove from oven and cool.

Mix glaze ingredients together until smooth; drizzle over top of lemon bars. Allow glaze to set. Cool bars completely before cutting into 15 squares.

Crust
1 cup (2 sticks) butter, softened
½ cup powdered sugar
½ tsp. salt
2 cups flour

Filling
4 eggs, beaten
2 cups sugar
½ tsp. baking powder
¼ cup flour
¼ cup lemon juice

Glaze
1 cup powdered sugar
2-3 tbl. lemon juice

153

Black Bottom Cupcakes

Topping

8 oz. cream cheese, softened
1 egg
⅓ cup sugar
1 cup (6 oz.) semi-sweet chocolate
   chips

Cakes

1½ cups flour
1 cup sugar
⅓ cup cocoa powder
1 tsp. baking soda
¼ tsp. salt
⅓ cup vegetable oil
1 tbl. vinegar
1 tsp. vanilla
1 cup cold water or strong coffee,
   cooled

Preheat oven to 350°

For topping: Beat cream cheese until smooth. Beat in sugar, then egg. Mix in chocolate chips. Set aside.

For cakes: Mix dry ingredients in medium mixing bowl. Make three wells in dry mixture. Put oil into one well, vinegar into the second, and vanilla into the third; it's OK if the liquid runs out of the wells. Pour the cold water or coffee over the whole thing and mix with a whisk until no lumps remain. Portion batter into muffin tins lined with cupcake liners, filling about ¾ full. Drop 2 tbl. of topping onto each cupcake. Bake for 15-20 minutes, just until tops of cakes are dry and tester inserted into cake part comes out dry.

Makes 24 cupcakes

154

Missy's Velvet Cheesecake

There are many different recipes for and ways to make cheesecake, and I've tried most of them. This is my favorite, and very easy.

Don't beat the filling too much – it adds air that will make the batter mound in the middle while baking and cause cracks in the top as it cools.

Preheat oven to 350°

Prepare pan: Turn a 10-inch springform pan upside down on counter. Cover outside bottom and sides with 2 layers of aluminum foil, pressing to ensure a tight fit. Turn pan over and spray inside with nonstick cooking spray.

Combine all crust ingredients well. Press evenly into bottom and up sides of prepared pan. Bake crust for 15 minutes, until lightly browned.

Beat cream cheese until smooth. Beat in sugar, scraping sides of bowl. Beat in eggs, one at a time, mixing well after each addition. Stir in sour cream and vanilla. Pour batter into crust. Place cake in a baking pan at least 1-inch larger all around. Fill pan halfway up sides with hot water. Carefully place in oven. Bake cake for 1¼ hours, until set when pan is lightly shaken.

Mix topping ingredients together until smooth. Spread over top of cheesecake. Bake for 15 minutes longer. Remove cake from oven, let cool to room temperature. Refrigerate several hours or overnight before serving.

You can make half a recipe in an 8-inch cake pan. Line the bottom of the pan with parchment before pressing the crust in. When the cake is cool, run a sharp knife around the edge to loosen the crust and turn it upside down on to a serving plate to remove the cake from the pan.

Crust

3 cups graham cracker crumbs
¾ cup sugar
¾ cup butter, melted

Filling

2 lbs. cream cheese
1 cup plus 5 tbl. sugar
4 eggs
1½ cups sour cream
2 tsp. vanilla extract

Topping

1½ cups sour cream
⅓ cup sugar
1 tsp. vanilla

Lime-Pineapple Pie

1 prepared 9-inch
graham cracker crust
8 oz. cream cheese
⅓ cup sugar
1 egg
½ cup canned crushed pineapple, drained
1 14-oz. can sweetened condensed milk
4 egg yolks
½ cup lime juice
Sweetened whipped cream for topping

Preheat oven to **350°**

Beat cream cheese until smooth. Beat in sugar, then egg. Stir in pineapple. Carefully spread mixture in bottom of pie crust. Whisk together condensed milk, egg yolks and lime juice. Pour over cream cheese mixture in crust. Bake for 20 minutes.

Remove from oven and let cool to room temperature, then refrigerate. Serve with whipped cream, if desired.

Chocolate Chip Cookie Pie

Preheat oven to 325°

In large bowl, beat eggs at high speed until foamy. Mix in butter. Beat in flour and both sugars until well blended. Stir in chocolate chips and walnuts. Pour into pie crust. Bake 55-60 minutes or until knife inserted halfway between center and edge comes out clean. Cool. Serve with whipped cream or ice cream, if desired.

Makes 6-8 servings

1 9-inch deep dish pie crust, unbaked
2 eggs
½ cup flour
½ cup sugar
½ cup packed brown sugar
1½ sticks butter, melted
1 cup pecans or walnuts, chopped
1 cup chocolate chips

Tastes like a chocolate chip cookie. Super easy and good!

Maple Rice Pudding

Place rice and milk in a large, heavy saucepan. Bring to a simmer over low heat. Simmer, uncovered, stirring occasionally for 25 - 30 minutes, until mixture has thickened. Stir in the maple syrup and dried fruit and simmer, stirring constantly, for 10 - 15 minutes longer. Stir in the vanilla, cinnamon, and nutmeg.

Spray an 8-inch square baking pan with nonstick cooking spray and pour the rice mixture into the dish. Cover tightly with aluminum foil. Bake for 20 minutes. Serve warm or cold.

Serves 6

2 cups cooked rice, preferably short- or long-grain brown rice
4 cups milk, rice milk, or soy milk
¾ cup maple syrup
⅓ cup dried cranberries, cherries, or raisins
1 tsp. vanilla extract
½ tsp. ground cinnamon
¼ tsp. ground nutmeg

Apple Crisp

Filling

8 medium crisp tart apples,
   peeled, cored and sliced
2 tbl. flour
2 tsp. lemon juice
¾ cup sugar
¾ tsp. cinnamon

Topping

6 tbl. (¾ stick) butter
¾ cup unbleached flour
½ cup plus 2 tbl. packed brown
   sugar
¾ cup old-fashioned or
   quick cooking
   rolled oats
   (not
   instant)

Preheat oven to 375°

In large bowl toss together all filling ingredients. Let sit for 5-10 minutes to let juices release from apples, stirring occasionally. Pour into a buttered 8-inch square pan.

Make topping: Mix all ingredients together with a hand mixer or in food processor until crumbly. Sprinkle topping evenly over apples. Bake at 375° for 45-60 minutes, until filling is bubbly and topping is golden brown.

Delicious served warm with vanilla ice cream.

Triple Chocolate Cake

Preheat oven to 350°

Spray three 8-inch round cake pans with nonstick cooking spray, line bottoms with parchment, spray again.

Mix dry ingredients in medium mixing bowl. Make three wells in dry mixture. Put oil into one well, vinegar into the second, and vanilla into the third; it's OK if the liquid runs out of the wells. Pour the cold water or coffee over the whole thing and mix with a whisk until no lumps remain. Pour batter evenly into prepared pans; bake for approx. 30 minutes, until tester inserted comes out clean. Cool in pans on rack 10 minutes, remove from pans and cool completely.

When cool, fill and frost layers with Cocoa Buttercream Icing.

Prepare Cocoa Buttercream Icing: Beat butter in mixing bowl until smooth and creamy. Add sugar, cocoa, milk and vanilla and mix until smooth. Spread between layers and over cooled cake. Press chopped chocolate chips into sides of cake.

Serves 10-12

3 cups all-purpose flour
2 cups sugar
⅔ cup cocoa powder
2 tsp. baking soda
¼ tsp. salt
⅔ cup vegetable oil
2 tbl. vinegar
1 tsp. vanilla
2 cups cold water or
    cooled strong coffee

Cocoa Buttercream Icing
12 tbl. (1½ sticks) butter, softened
4 cups powdered sugar
1 cup cocoa powder
6-8 tbl. milk
2 tsp. vanilla
1½ cups chocolate chips, chopped

Velvet Chocolate Cake

Cake

2½ cups unbleached white flour
or 3¼ cups barley flour
1¾ cups turbinado sugar
½ cup unsweetened cocoa
powder
1 tsp. baking soda
½ cup melted butter or
soft Spectrum spread
¾ cup canola oil
1 cup buttermilk or Silk soymilk
creamer
3 large eggs or ¾
cup silken style
tofu, drained and
mashed
1 tsp. salt
2 tsp. vanilla

Chocolate Glaze

¼ cup fine quality
unsweetened
cocoa
¼ cup cream or
Silk soymilk
creamer
1 tsp. vanilla extract
1¾ cups powdered
sugar and sift after
measuring

Preheat oven to 350°

Spray a bundt pan with nonstick vegetable spray and dust with flour.

Place unsifted flour, sugar, cocoa, baking soda, salt and melted butter or substitute in a 3 quart saucepan and heat over low heat slowly until ingredients are just incorporated, 2 to 3 minutes.

Transfer to mixer bowl and add the oil, buttermilk or soy creamer, vanilla and eggs or tofu. Beat at medium speed for 2 minutes or until well blended. Pour into the prepared Bundt pan and bake at 350° for 35 to 40 minutes or until a toothpick inserted comes out clean.

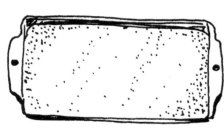

Cool 5 minutes then remove from cake from pan.

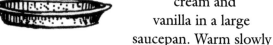

While cake is baking, prepare the glaze by placing cocoa, cream and vanilla in a large saucepan. Warm slowly to melt the chocolate. Remove from heat and beat in the powdered sugar. Pour glaze over slightly cooled cake.

Lemon Crumb Cake

Preheat oven to 350°

Lightly butter and flour 8-inch square baking dish. Stir flour, both sugars, lemon zest and cinnamon in large bowl to blend. Add oil and lemon juice and stir until mixture is combined and forms clumps.

Set aside 1 cup for topping.

Place yogurt, egg, vanilla, baking powder and baking soda in mixer bowl and beat until blended. Add crumb mixture and beat until batter is smooth. Spread in prepared pan and sprinkle reserved crumbs over top. Bake for 40 minutes, or until tester inserted comes out clean. Sift powdered sugar over top when cool.

Serves 8 - 12

2 cups unbleached flour
1 cup sugar
½ cup golden brown sugar
4 tsp. grated lemon zest
¾ tsp. cinnamon
6 tbl. canola oil
2 tbl. fresh lemon juice
1 cup nonfat plain yogurt
1 large egg
1 tsp. vanilla extract
1¾ tsp. baking powder
¼ tsp. baking soda

Excellent at tea-time with some friends . . .

Tofu Chocolate Silk Pie

This pie is rich, chocolatey and delicious!

1 9-inch graham cracker crust
1 12-oz. package (2 cups) malted chocolate chips
1 10.5 oz. brick silken-style soft tofu, room temperature
2 tbl. honey or maple syrup

Melt chocolate chips in a double boiler over low heat, or in a microwave on high for 1 minute, stirring to finish melting. Place tofu in bowl of food processor or blender jar (an electric mixer may be used) and blend until creamy and smooth. Add melted chocolate in four parts, blending well after each addition. Add honey or maple syrup to taste. Pour filling into graham cracker crust and refrigerate several hours. Garnish with whipped cream if desired.

Serves 6 - 8

Pumpkin Pie

Preheat oven to 450°

Beat eggs and both sugars together until light. Stir in pumpkin puree, spices, salt and mix thoroughly. Stir in cream and half-and-half. Pour filling into pie shell.

Bake the pie at 450° for 8 minutes, then reduce heat to 325° and bake for another 40 - 45 minutes, or until filling is set (a knife inserted in the center will come out clean). Remove pie to rack to cool. Allow pie to cool completely before cutting.

Serves 8

3 eggs (OR ¾ cup Eggbeaters)
⅓ cup granulated sugar or fructose
⅓ cup brown sugar
2 cups canned pumpkin puree
1 teaspoon ground ginger
1½ teaspoons ground cinnamon
1 teaspoon ground allspice
¼ tsp. salt
¾ cup heavy cream
¾ cup half-and-half (OR 1½ cups nonfat evaporated milk)
1 9-inch deep dish pie crust, unbaked

moon light through oak tree
full moon
July 15, 2000

Around the World Cookies

3 cups spelt flour
1½ cups turbinado sugar
1½ cups Yellow "D" sugar or
  brown sugar
2 tsp. baking soda
½ tsp. salt
1 stick (½ cup) butter, melted
3 eggs
1 tbl. vanilla

1 cup chocolate chips
1 cup coconut flakes
1 cup pecans, chopped
1 cup raisins

Vegetable spray

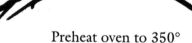

Preheat oven to 350°

In a large bowl mix the dry
ingredients, making sure baking soda is
free of lumps.

Mix the wet ingredients together, add to dry
ingredients and stir. Add chocolate chips, coconut
flakes, pecans and raisins and mix (using your hands
sometimes gets the best results). Prepare cookie
sheets with vegetable spray. Measure 3 tbl. of dough
and form a ball. Place balls 3 inches apart on
prepared cookie sheet, flatten slightly. Bake for
12-15 minutes, until lightly browned
and puffed.

Makes 15 giant cookies

Low-fat Cheesecake

Preheat oven to 300°

Line bottom of a 9-inch springform pan with parchment or waxed paper. Spray bottom and sides with nonstick cooking spray. In food processor, process granola until it forms fine crumbs. Coat pan with granola, rotating so crumbs cover the bottom and sides evenly.

Place cottage cheese, sour cream and cream cheese in bowl of food processor. Process until mixture is very smooth and creamy. Add honey or sugar, cornstarch, eggs, egg whites and lemon zest. Process until well combined and smooth.

Pour filling into prepared pan, smoothing top. Bake for 55 minutes. Cake will be firm at the edges but wobbly in the center. Turn oven off and leave cheesecake in oven with door closed for 30 minutes longer. Remove from oven and let cool on rack. Refrigerate for several hours or overnight. Remove sides from pan before serving. Top with fresh fruit, if desired.

Serves 12

Nonstick cooking spray

¼ cup low fat granola

16 oz. nonfat cottage cheese

1½ cups nonfat sour cream

12 oz. reduced fat cream cheese, softened

¾ cup honey, or 1¼ cups sugar or fructose

6 tbl. cornstarch

2 large eggs

2 egg whites

2 tsp. finely grated lemon zest (yellow part only)

Mixed Fruit Cobbler

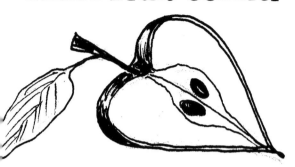

5 firm apples, such as Royal Gala
   or Golden Delicious
4 peaches, or 1½ cups frozen
1 cup fresh or frozen blueberries
2 tbl. flour
⅓ cup honey or 6 tbl. fructose
1 tsp. lemon juice

Topping
2 cups flour
3 tbl. honey or ¼ cup packed
   Yellow "D" sugar or brown
   sugar
2 tsp. baking powder
6 tbl. cold butter or margarine
¾ cup plus 2 tbl. whipping cream

Preheat oven to 375°

Peel and core apples;
cut into ¼-inch slices.
Peel and pit peaches;
cut into ¼-inch slices. Place apples, peaches
and blueberries in a large bowl. Add flour,
honey or fructose, and lemon juice. Mix
gently and place in a buttered 2 quart
ovenproof baking dish.

For topping: combine flour, honey or sugar,
and baking powder in a mixer bowl. Add
butter and mix on low speed until butter is
in ¼-inch pieces. Slowly add ¾ cup cream
while continuing to mix just until combined.
Place dough on a lightly floured board and
roll ½-inch thick. Using a 3-inch round, star
or heart-shaped cutter, cut the dough into
shapes and place them on top of the fruit
filling. Brush the tops of the dough shapes
with the remaining 2 tablespoons of cream.
Bake the cobbler for 25 - 30 minutes, until
the filling is bubbling and the top is golden
brown. Serve with vanilla ice cream or
whipped cream.

Serves 8

So perfect Hot
right out of the oven

Squash Pie

Preheat oven to 450°

Prepare crust: In food processor, place flour and butter in work bowl. Pulse on and off until mixture resembles corn meal. Add water with machine running, blending just until dough forms a ball. Do not overmix. On a floured surface, roll crust out to 1/8-inch thickness, and line a 9-inch pie plate with it. Trim and crimp crust to form a tall edge around rim of pie.

Place squash in a blender or food processor. Add eggs, honey or maple syrup, and spices. Blend until squash is pureed. Add half-and-half and blend until well mixed. Pour filling into pie shell. Bake at 450° for 8 minutes, then reduce heat to 325° and bake for another 40 - 45 minutes, until a knife inserted in the center of filling comes out clean. Cool and serve chilled or at room temperature. Great with a spoonful of whipped cream on top.

Makes 8 servings

Crust

1¾ cups whole wheat or
  unbleached flour
½ cup (1 stick) cold butter
5 tbl. cold water

Filling

2 cups cooked butternut squash
  (about 1-1½ lbs.) *Cut squash in
  half, scoop out seeds and place
  cut-side down on lightly greased
  baking sheet. Bake at 350 for 30-
  45 minutes, until soft.*
3 eggs
½ cup honey or ⅔ cup maple
  syrup
1 tsp. ground ginger
1½ tsp. ground cinnamon
½ tsp. ground allspice
Pinch salt
1½ cups half-and-half

Zucchini Pineapple Cake

3 eggs
1½ cups honey
2 tsp. vanilla
1 cup vegetable oil
3 cups unbleached flour
1 tsp. baking powder
1 tsp. baking soda
½ tsp. salt
1½ tsp. ground cinnamon
½ tsp. allspice
2 cups finely grated zucchini
1 cup (1 8-oz. can) crushed
   pineapple with juice
1 cup pecans or walnuts,
   chopped
Cream Cheese Icing,
   page 139

Preheat oven to 350. Spray 3 9-inch round cake pans with nonstick vegetable spray, line bottoms with baking parchment, spray again and sprinkle with flour. Set aside.

Beat eggs, honey, vanilla, and oil in large mixing bowl. Mix in flour, baking powder, baking soda, salt and spices until no lumps remain. Stir in zucchini, pineapple with juice, and nuts.

Pour batter into prepared pans. Place on middle rack of oven and bake for 25 minutes, or until tester inserted comes out clean. Cool in pans for 10 minutes, remove from pans and place on cooling racks until cool. Fill and frost layers with Cream Cheese Icing.

Makes 1 9-inch layer cake

Leaves

Woodland stem

LEUCOJUM AESTIUM
"Gravetye Ceiaut"

Raspberry Marzipan Tart

Preheat oven to 350°

Place almonds and orange zest in bowl of food processor fitted with a knife blade and process until almonds are finely ground but not ground to a paste. Add butter and process until smooth, scraping down sides of workbowl. Add sugar, orange juice, eggs and almond extract and process until well mixed, scraping down sides of bowl occasionally.

Spread raspberry preserves evenly over bottom of prepared tart shell. Scrape filling into tart shell and spread evenly with a rubber spatula. Bake for 40 - 45 minutes, until filling is slightly puffed and brown, and is set when pan is lightly shaken. Cool on wire rack. Sprinkle tart with powdered sugar when cool.

Makes 8 slices

1 unbaked tart shell in 9-inch low-sided fluted tart pan with removable bottom
1½ cups slivered or sliced blanched almonds
½ tsp. orange zest, finely grated (orange part only of orange peel)
½ cup (1 stick) butter
½ cup granulated sugar
3 tbl. orange juice
2 eggs
½ tsp. natural almond extract
⅓ cup raspberry preserves

Fresh Lemon Tart

1 unbaked tart shell in 9-inch high-sided fluted quiche pan with removable bottom
½ cup (1 stick) butter, softened
1⅓ cups granulated sugar
2 tbl. cornstarch
5 eggs
2 egg yolks
1 cup fresh lemon juice
1½ tsp. vanilla
¼ tsp. salt
1 tsp. lemon zest, finely grated (yellow part only of lemon peel)

Preheat oven to 400°

Line tart shell with foil; place 1 cup of dried beans or pie weights in foil to keep crust from puffing during baking. Place in preheated oven and bake for 10 minutes. Remove from oven, remove foil from pan and reduce oven heat to 350°.

Beat butter, sugar and cornstarch in mixing bowl until light and fluffy. Beat in eggs, one at a time, then egg yolks, scraping down sides of bowl occasionally. Mix in lemon juice, vanilla, salt and lemon zest. Mixture may separate or look curdled – this is OK. Pour filling into tart shell. Place in oven and bake for 40-45 minutes, until filling is set when pan is gently shaken. Remove from oven to cool. Sprinkle top of tart with powdered sugar when cool. Cut into 8-10 wedges.

Maple Oat Squares
Wheat-Free & Dairy-Free

Preheat oven to 350°

Line an 8-inch square baking pan with aluminum foil. Butter foiled pan and set aside.

Place the butter, sugar, and maple syrup in a medium saucepan. Stir over low heat until butter melts and mixture comes to a low boil. Remove from heat. Stir in oats and nuts. Pour mixture into prepared pan and even the top with the back of a spoon, pressing firmly.

Bake until light golden brown, about 25-30 minutes. Let cool completely before cutting into 1½-inch squares.

Makes about 25

½ cup butter or margarine
¼ cup firmly packed Yellow "D" sugar or brown sugar
5 tbl. maple syrup
2 cups baby or quick-cooking oats
½ cup whole almonds, chopped
½ cup hazelnuts, chopped

"Failure is the key to success - each mistake teaches us something." —Morihei Ueshiba

Love Always Perseveres

Perseverance is a character builder, which strengthens us and allows us the realization of "do we really love who or what we love." The difficulties which might present themselves are not obstacles preventing us to move towards the fulfillment of our hopes. Yet, the heart remains open to reason and divine guidance thus surrendering our will. In our determination to obtain our goal, it is of valuable use that we proceed with great care, our perseverance should not become stubbornness, which will move us into a state of immobility, where love and grace are blocked. This state creates a closing off of other possibilities: blindness disguised as perseverance. The heart of perseverance is a willingness to suffer the desert places one must traverse yet not get stuck in our own willfulness. The Promised Land is there and we must MOVE in faith to get there.

When we try out recipes, perseverance is useful. It will allow for moving through a tough spot. For instance, the sauce gets stuck at the bottom of the pan but is not yet burned. With a little perseverance we can transfer it into another pot and proceed more carefully or adjust the ingredients according to the problem. Too little fluid or the flame too high. We may realize that an ingredient is missing in the pantry. So, instead of giving up on the dish we add a little of our own creativity to the recipe. Stubbornness would proceed with a much less inventive manner such as pretending that it will not burn with out any adjustments.

Anne

Miscellaneous

"I don't like 'this' cooking or 'that' cooking. I like 'good' cooking."
—James Beard

Blackening Spice

For chicken, meat, fish and grilled veggies.

2½ tbl. paprika
1 tbl. sea salt
1 tbl. thyme
1 tbl. rubbed sage
½ tbl. cayenne pepper
1½ tbl. granulated garlic
1½ tbl. dried onion
1½ tbl. dried basil
1½ tbl. yellow dried mustard
½ tbl. black pepper
½ tbl. crushed red chili peppers
½ tbl. Italian herbs

Pour all the spices in a jar with lid and shake well.
Store in a cool dark place.

Moroccan Spice Blend

2 tbl. cumin
3 tbl. ground coriander
3 tbl. turmeric
1½ tbl. ground cinnamon
1 tsp. salt
1 tsp. nutmeg

Shake together to mix.

Hummus

2 15-oz. cans garbanzo beans,
    drain one
¼ cup roasted tahini
4 large cloves garlic, peeled
2 tbl. extra virgin olive oil
Juice of 2 lemons
½ cup chopped cilantro
1 tsp. salt
½ tsp. ground cumin

Place all ingredients in a food processor and puree. Add salt to taste.

Serve with bread, pita, crackers or tortilla chips.

Tofu Hummus

1 lb. firm tofu
¼ cup toasted sesame tahini
2 large cloves garlic
½ tsp. ground cumin
½ tsp. salt
½ cup chopped cilantro
2 to 3 tbl. fresh squeezed lemon
    juice
½ tsp. cayenne (optional)

Puree all the ingredients in a food processor to a thick paste or hummus.

Serve with bread, pita, crackers or corn chips.

Makes 2½ cups

Tofu and Roasted Red Pepper Dip

3 red bell peppers seeded, membranes removed
1 16-oz. cake firm tofu
¼ cup olive oil
5 cloves garlic
½ cup tahini
½ cup cilantro chopped
1/3 cup fresh lemon juice
½ tsp. cumin
Salt to taste

Pre heat oven to 400°

Place bell peppers cut side down on a greased baking sheet. Roast about 20 minutes or until they are turning brown and the skins are blistering. Immediately place the peppers in a plastic bag to cool. Remove the skins (this can be done under running water but it will remove some flavor).

Combine all the ingredients in a food processor fitted with the steel blade and puree until a smooth paste forms.

Taste and adjust. For a more lemony taste add more juice, etc....

Good protein source. Delicious party dip.

Moroccan Mint Tea

2 teabags black tea
5 cups boiling water
20 small fresh mint sprigs, rinsed
Sugar or honey to taste

Place teabags into your favorite teapot, pour boiling water over them. Let steep for a few minutes. Press all the mint into the teapot and sweeten.

Serve hot.

4 to 6 servings